FROM UNDER THE CLOUD

Personal Reminiscences of Insanity

BY ANNA AGNEW

Originally Published in 1886
Cincinnati: Robert Clarke & Co.

Dedication.

This Volume is Affectionately Dedicated
TO
MY CHILDREN,

Pittsburg, Penn.,

April 26, 1886.

"My heart will still cling to them fondly,
And dream of sweet memories past;
While hope, like the rainbow of promise,
Gives assurance of meeting at last."

PREFACE.

In attempting a history of a very painful period of my life, I recognize the difficulty under which I shall labor, particularly in the account given of the time spent at the hospital for insane. In my efforts to give a perfectly truthful account of occurrences there, I wish particularly to impress upon the public the fact that I have not the slightest intention or inclination to reflect upon the three different managements under whose care I was during a period of seven years, as I could have not one word to say against their personal kindness to myself, or any other patient — but at the same time, will speak freely of gross abuses, for which there is no remedy, until state laws require that none but those who are fitted for the sacred duties of attendants upon the insane be employed — such preparation being a complete course in a training school for nursing.

I say, fearlessly, that I am competent to judge of the wisdom of such requirement, and from painful experience consider it my duty to speak in behalf of my suffering sisters. Superintendents should not be held responsible for unfaithful attendants — for to no person is this class so obsequious, so invariably upon their good behavior, as before this officer. One of our superintendents in an article on this subject says: "The wards of the insane are a sealed book to the superintendent," and even he, though particularly watchful for the comfort of the unfortunate inmates, realizes very slightly the full meaning of his term, "sealed book."

"Nothing extenuate nor set down aught in malice." Let this be my aim. And so I send out my book, freighted with many an anxious, troubled thought from the retrospective glances of a saddened life; trusting sincerely that its many faults may be treated with leniency, and its merits, if so be any are discovered, generously appreciated.

Sincerely,

Anna Agnew.

Pittsburg, Penn.,

April 26, 1886.

The author wishes to express publicly her earnest thanks to the gentlemen who have so kindly given her permission to use their letters of congratulation to her, as testimonials to her publishers, also for their photos, which she much regrets not being able to insert, recognizing as she does, the value of such marks of esteem and favor as giving character to her literary effort, not only from the high standing of the gentlemen personally, but also as authorities of pronounced prominence among experts on insanity.

CHAPTER I.

> Of all sad words, by tongue or pen,
> The saddest are these: "It *might* have been." — Whittier.

I KNOW of four *other* words far sadder; and fearful, too, because of their truth and finality: "It *was* to be." It might *not* have been, or it would be. "It was to be," and it *will* be, beyond the shadow of a doubt. And there is another *single* word — to me the most fearful and suggestive in the English language, when put in the form of interrogation — the simple little word, Why? It is so often, so cruelly unanswerable. Psychologists tell us of persons born with what they style an insane temperament; but that the possession of this unfortunate temperament is not necessarily followed by insanity. Circumstances may rule in their favor. Their surroundings may be so peaceful, their lives so protected, that their latent insanity need never develop farther than to cause them to be classed among the large number of peculiar people whom we all meet in daily life, whose peculiarities only cause a smile.

In a degree this may be true., and I am not inclined to question its scientific phase. But may not the simply peculiar trait of the parent, develop into insanity in the child? I do not believe that circumstances are *accidents* in any of our lives; and, instead of being "creatures of circumstances," I believe circumstances are *created*, as necessary for the fulfillment of the plan marked out for each mortal from the beginning — my belief being born of experience such as falls to the lot of few, fortunately. If it were not so — if we could choose our path — would any one deliberately choose misery? We walk where we must, not where, or as, we will; and *my* steps *tended* toward the *insane asylum* from my cradle.

I presume I am one in whom the insane temperament predominates, in a marked degree, since, in a retrospective view of my life almost to infancy, I can recall many peculiarities of character not usual in children — aspirations and longings, repeated attempts at accomplishing things beyond childish attainment, with their consequent failures. And I can recall days of gloom — when too young yet to have even heard of the traditional "silver lined clouds" — the memory of which, even now, makes me shudder, that a child should be so hopeless, even for one moment!

I think I was born with a suicidal tendency; and in every trouble of my life, real or fancied, this was my predominant impulse — the hope by this means of escaping from an impatiently borne life. And I do not remember the time, when opportunity suggested the trial — such as standing upon an elevation, or being upon water of sufficient depth, that I had not to exercise the utmost strength of will to control the impulse to then and there cross the invisible line, and be free from the tormenting, persistent feeling of pursuit and unrest. To escape, if possible, from the terrible shadowy something constantly haunting me, whose influence made itself felt in my happiest moments, giving character even to my dreams, and whose climax was insanity! I often wonder, *now*, if my life might not have been different — surely it would have been *brighter* — had there been some one to whom I could have unbosomed myself; to whom I could have talked freely of these shadows that so oppressed me; some one who would not, at the sight of my frequent tears, have chilled my attempted confidences with words of cold censure, instead of encouragement. I don't know that it would have materially changed my life; possibly it may have given me something pleasant to remember of my childhood — a boon I have to regret I do not possess. But there was no such comfort for me! I was a proud, willful, and not always an obedient child. But to my father never intentionally *disobedient* or *disrespectful*.

And from him I inherited my most pronounced traits of character, hence my inclination to confide in him more than in any other person. And I do not remember that I ever went to him for sympathy that he did not try to lighten my burden (often an imaginary one, I must admit), instead of, on the contrary, reminding me that it was "my own fault, my own ugly temper," and so on — phrases grown so familiar from frequent repetition as to be heard and treated with contempt. It was *not* my own fault! It is no child's fault that it is cursed with an unhappy disposition . hbat greater misfortune could befall a child? And it would be well, indeed, for parents to look well into their own hearts and lives for the cause, before they disown any trait in their children, be it ever so unpleasant. From my soul I pity the child whose predominant memory is of being considered the odd sheep in the family flock! The mysterious stranger, who got his or her disposition from the "Lord knows where, or whom!" — neither parent being willing to shoulder the disagreeable responsibility.

I wonder of whom I got my pride. And I wonder greatly of *what* I was proud. In imagination I can see my father's troubled face, and hear his anxious voice, as he said once to me, when I — then a young girl — was giving utterance to some grievance in an emphatic manner: "Mark my word, my daughter! Your pride will be brought low, before you die. I hope not to live to see it, but you will some time remember my words!" And have I *not* had reason to remember them in bitterest anguish? And I *know* I am glad, and thankful, *too*, that he was spared witnessing his daughter's humiliation.

I hope my readers will understand that I am not inclined to censure any one, or charge them with being the cause of my insanity. I have no such intention. I place the responsibility exactly where it belongs. The *Almighty* controls such matters. We are *his* creatures, utterly helpless in his hands. And, however we may struggle and grow desperate in our efforts to *reconcile* the directly opposite attributes, those of a "kind and merciful Father, who pities our infirmities," "who never willingly afflicts his children," "whose cross is not too heavy to be borne," with the same Father who speaks us into existence, bearing within us traits that must ripen into a harvest fearful beyond words to express. And, though his promises are that we shall *not* be tried beyond our strength, that the back *shall* be fitted for the burden, *does* desert us in our extremity. Let those who have never thus been so fearfully tried reconcile these inconsistencies, *if they can*; and love the One who embodies them, *if they choose*. I do not care to enter into a controversy of the matter; but, at the same time, *do* claim the right to question his methods, and the *instruments* used.

My stock, *originally*, of the commodity, "*unquestioning faith*," was limited to a small amount; and years and experience have not increased it. I have learned, by bitter sorrow, the fallacy of trusting even the promises of God. Implicit faith in anybody, or any thing, is a thing of the past; and its absence is not greatly regretted. I believe I am *happier* since; certainly I am more content.

I remember that I used to dwell with horror upon the bible-inspired thought of being left to myself! given up! Of the spirit taking its everlasting flight! and numerous other terrible threatenings. And no thought gave me such horror as the possibility of endless torment after death, in spite of earnest effort to live correctly. Such doubts and fears trouble me no longer; for, of *this* I am certain, this life nor the hereafter holds nothing, for me, worse than the past! The very bitterest cup that malignant fate holds for mortals, *I* have drank to the *last drop*! Friendless and alone, I have fought this *demon*, insanity! and have come *out*, strengthened for whatever the future holds for me. And one bright hope it has — that of being reunited to my children, when they shall have become the noble *men* their *youth promises*. As for the next world, I feel not the slightest anxiety. I have passed through a "furnace of affliction" such as few are called upon to endure; and, whether the dross in my nature be purified or not, there 's no depth of misery I have not sounded. And where is the theologian who can successfully *refute* my *sincere belief,* that insanity is the *real hell* spoken of in the Bible?

> Dear as remembered kisses after death,
> And sweet as those by hopeless fancy feigned,
> Oh lips that are for others! Deep as love —
> Deep as first love — and wild with all regret,
> Oh Death in life, the days that are no morel
> — Tennyson

CHAPTER II.

This truth came home with bier and pall,
I felt it when I sorrowed most:
'Tis better to have loved and lost,
Than never to have loved at all.
—Whittier.

My readers must not infer, from the preceding chapter, that I
was an *altogether* unhappy girl; for, indeed, such was far from
being the fact. Few persons, I think, possessed a keener sense
of enjoyment, or had brighter hours, than I, only they were not
uniformly so—and unusual gayety was too frequently
followed by melancholy. I was a passionate lover of music, as
I am still, and was strangely moved by it often to tears, and at
times, too, when such effect was embarrassing. And, now, the
slight knowledge of it is a *real blessing*—acting as a sort of
safety valve to repressed feeling, too deep, often, for words.
So, when my dark days come—for they do yet come,
sometimes—I strike a few chords, and sing my useless regrets
away. And my attachments were strong and *lasting*, while
their *object* remained faithful, not longer.

I have but little reverence for traditions-*simply as traditions*.
Indeed, a phrenologist told me once that, instead of a bump,
there was a reverential depression on my head. So, it is not
surprising, that my really sincere expressions, directly
opposite to cherished traditions, sometimes jar upon sensitive
ears, and cause even looks of pained surprise from those
whom I would not willingly wound.

I do not readily forget! and I make no effort to *forget*,
injuries—"let the dead rest." Why, if the dead have willfully,
cruelly wronged us, Death is our common lot—and there are
sorrows to which, by comparison, death is a blessing. I think,
honestly, I used to endeavor to shape my life, as regards my

dealings with my fellows, by the "golden rule," until forced by experience into changing the wording (since the substance so often failed me) to suit my own individuality. And I find that, doing unto others, as others do, and have done, unto me, works quite as satisfactorily — and does not so often give one the heartache, as the unexpected violation of the original rule was wont to do. Those who *prefer* the old path, however, need not be disturbed by my departure. And, since faith is so beautiful, I would be sorry to say one word to disturb any one possessing it.

When I was married, I sincerely loved my husband! And my children were my idols — I almost worshiped them! And, until this *trouble* came, I was happier, more contented, than in all my previous life. I must say trouble, yet it was not "domestic trouble!" I do not *now*, and never *have*, held my husband responsible for my affliction, in any *intentional* manner. The "domestic trouble phase" was of recent date. I am glad to have the memory of a pleasant, comfortable, *peaceful home* — the few years I was permitted to enjoy it. And when comparing, as I am obliged truthfully to do, my husband as he *was then* (thoughtful and careful of my comfort ever), *with the man* who, only a few months since, refused me even the privilege of *seeing* our children, and brutally bade me "go to the Knox county *poor-house* for support," rather than into his house and the society of our children, it is small wonder that I feel I have but *recently* formed his real acquaintance — and the fact that, for five years or more, I thought my husband a *gentleman,* must be sadly laid away among other kindred "delusions." Why was I not, after such a heartless repulse, driven back into the shadow — worse than death — from which I had so recently emerged? "It was *not* to be." The last *voluntary* act of my life — before the blow came — was for the comfort of my family. On the night of November — nineteenth — seventy-six — I sat sewing upon a garment for one of my children, until quite late, but put it away not quite done! And I never finished it!

Something had come over me! I wakened the following Sunday morning, bathed in a cold, clammy perspiration, with an inexpressibly horrible sensation, as though falling—falling into some dreadful place of darkness! I had not the strength to speak, or move! And a cold, shadowy something seemed settling down upon me—indescribable, but altogether horrible!

When fully awake, I recognized my condition! For the second time within the year I was *completely helpless* from "nervous prostration!" And, startling as a flash of lightning in a clear sky, came the *revelation*, this *"something!"* that had been with me *all my life!* walking by my side! invisible, but *felt* even in my *happiest moments!* haunting me, and threatening to overwhelm me at some unexpected, happy moment, had come! and it was *insanity!*

And *then* it was, as has so heartlessly been said of me, "I deliberately folded my hands, and announced my intention of being sick." My hands *were* folded! my work taken *out* of *them!* But it was not *I* did it! They were busy, *helping* hands before! A power *stronger than mine* made them *helpless!* They were *horribly folded*—and for six miserable years only busied themselves in fruitless attempts to end my wretched existence. All life, all beauty, all *brightness* was gone from me! And *yet* I could not die! Oh! ye whose hearts are tender, pity me! Mothers! all over this land, in your sheltered, peaceful homes! try and imagine the depths of my sorrow. Look at your *own little ones!* Gather them into your arms; and, if you have faith in the power of prayer to avert the curses the Almighty *surely sends* upon his helpless creatures, then pray more earnestly than ever you petitioned blessings, that this most terrible of afflictions come not to *your* hearthstone.

I know I *once* had faith in His promises. "Let not your hearts be troubled; ye believe in God, believe also in me," was to my troubled, but trusting soul, as "the shadow of a great rock in a weary land." As I prepared myself for church on the above-mentioned Sunday morning, every breath was a prayer for help or comfort. But no comfort came! The sermon, and walk home, seemed a confused and troubled dream! Until just as we reached home, my little son, whom I had taken with me, stepped forward to open the gate, and said, "Mamma, aren't you glad to have a big boy *like* me to take you to church, when papa's not at home?" And I said, "No, Dadie! mamma don't feel as though she could ever be *glad again — of any thing!*" Dear little fellow! he was *only six years old.* Shall I ever forget his troubled, perplexed look, as he said, "Why won't you *never* be glad again, mamma?" Little child as he was, he felt the difference in my manner; and I hope he remembers yet how his mamma *used* to take him *in her arms* and, with kisses, tell him how glad she was, and *proud, too,* that she *had* such a "big boy" to take care of her, and to *love.* He was a jealous little boy; and, in my imagination, I can still hear him saying, with a sort of doubtful expression, "Course [of course] you love my two little *brothers*! And you *ought* to, mamma! for they's your little boys, *too*! But you love me *best*! *Course you do*! for I'm your *first baby.*" Another little childish utterance of his stays with me like a prophecy. His brother, younger than he, was constantly talking of when he was to be married, and Dadie said, "Well, I'm *never* going to get married. I'll stay at home, and board with my mamma!"

Does any *mother* doubt that I love my children? I was with them such a *little while*! And I think I can recall more of their sweet, childish sayings, than most mothers. In the daily cares and duties of life, when our children are around us, many bright sayings of the little ones pass from our memory. But I had so many years to think, when there was nothing left me *but* memory; and, though sadly realizing that —

> "'Tis the truth, the poet sings,
> That a sorrower's crown of sorrow,
> Is remembering happier things,"

I am glad *my* memory was not blotted out, my memories are *not all bitter*! And yet, upon this child's account, I am branded, upon the hospital records, with a name worse than that of murderess! It is shameful and cruel in the extreme, that I am recorded "homicidal." Suicidal I was, in thought and intention, for years! But no thought of *murder* was in my heart when attempting the deed that consigned me to the "asylum for the insane." On the contrary, it was an effort to save my child from the fearful (possible) heritage of *insanity*! And my desperation was intensified by cruel insinuation, and vile, abusive taunts, from those surrounding me, whose public professions were of sympathy, but whose private acts were those of *fiends*! I reasoned thus (for insane persons *do* reason, sometimes fearfully to the point, too): That it were far better that I lay all my little ones at rest, than they live to become victims of a fate than which *death* is a positive, *welcome guest*. That was my horror *then!* But I do not fear that fate for them now. Insanity was not my inheritance! Only the peculiar tendency in that direction was inherited. And my complete recovery, with not one single faculty dimmed, but on the contrary strengthened and brightened, proves my trouble to have been simply local, which, with skillful treatment, such as few are favored with, *completed the cure*! A change from brutality *to* kindness began it, and insanity is becoming every year better understood — and though there may be an inherent tendency in that direction, science and the surroundings may combat if not entirely prevent it.

CHAPTER. III.

A little learning is a dangerous thing;
Drink deep, or taste not the Pierian spring.
There shallow draughts intoxicate the brain,
And drinking largely sobers us again.
—Pope.

I AM now approaching a period of time, the recollection of which causes more profound sadness than any other period of my affliction. Unfortunately, for all concerned, I was not taken to the asylum for a period of several years after the time when common sense, if not common humanity, should have decided that such was the only proper place for me. Right here let me implore those persons so unfortunate as to have friends needing such restraint, not to cherish the old-timed, ignorant idea of some thing *disgraceful* being attached to this form of affliction; and above all, keep from the *stricken one* the shadow of reflection that they have disgraced their family since *they* are insane. The bitterest, most indignant feelings toward my friends were born of this very thought. I sincerely believe that the miserable record of those years, the impressions *made* and *received* by me, when my case was so cruelly, or ignorantly, which? misunderstood outside of the asylum, made seven years inside of its walls a necessity, for which I must hold my immediate family, in a measure, responsible, granting at the same time, they intended kindness to me in keeping me home. But I was neither treated as an insane, nor yet wholly responsible woman. Often, not with the consideration shown a willful child. At times charged with being a hypocrite. Of feigning insanity to evade the responsibilities of my home duties. Of acting the fool. Of simply having the devil in me, The latter being the openly expressed opinion of the "head of the medical profession" in the historical old town of *Vincennes*, Indiana. I, the victim, and

13

so considered sinner, in the meantime, was devoting every energy I possessed to one single idea, that of escaping from all this horror by taking my own life. I expect a humane, charitable public to believe in my sincerity, while I attempt to give them my strange experience, and they may explain, if they can, *why* I could not succeed in my suicidal attempts. And I beg most earnestly to be believed when I say, most *positively*, I am *not* writing these facts for sensational effect. I trust they may serve to prevent other similar misconceptions of " peculiar" condition and actions of unfortunates such as I. After having already, at different times, swallowed an ounce of laudanum, four ounces of a preparation of chloral, the regular dose of which was one teaspoonful, a tablespoonful of pulverized sugar of lead, which latter thoroughly poisoned me until my tongue, throat and stomach were in ulcers — I repeat, after having swallowed *all these*, I threw myself upon the mercy of two prominent physicians who were called in consultation upon my case, telling them I was all the time tempted to kill myself, and was afraid I might hurt some one else, and I begged for their advice. In return for my sincere confidence, this brutal remark was made: "You might put a quart of poison on that mantlepiece with perfect safety. Persons who are contemplating suicide don't advertise the fact." Some months later, these same gentlemen (?) were called to attend me after I had swallowed *strychnine* in sufficient quantity to "kill an elephant, if properly ad ministered," as the druggist from whom I bought it said, when he sold it to me for the purpose of killing rats. One of these physicians, "the head," saw me at the beginning of the case, when every nerve was convulsively twitching, and with the remark that it was perfectly wonderful what had gotten me into such a *nervous state*. But he rather guessed it was *hysteria*, gave me a dose of "bromide of potassium," and left quite a quantity *to* be given. Nervous! great Heavens! I was in fearful *convulsions* five minutes after his prescription and departure! The other one called after the convulsions had spent their strength; the recurrent spasms, each somewhat lighter at intervals of perhaps ten minutes, my body and lower limbs perfectly rigid, in which condition they remained for twenty-four hours without the slightest relaxation. And *he*, after an examination, and with the wise look of an *owl in daylight*, guessed it was — shades of Aesculapius, listen — *worms*! and he *prescribed* accordingly. I am the possessor of an old, valued, \Yell-read copy of Charles Reid's "Hard Cash." I don't care to part with it, but for the sake of *humanity*, will present it to those *two gentlemen* as splendid authority upon the *symptoms* of strychnine poisoning. Oh! not at all, gentlemen! No thanks are necessary! You are entirely welcome! One of these persons, the *worm specialist*, signed the papers presented to the commission, appointed to decide as to whether or no I was a subject for the asylum, and I presume made *oath* to his opinion, that I was *insane*, else the asylum authorities would not have accepted the application for my admission there as a patient — but at the same time informed my husband that the *penitentiary* was the more suitable place, and advised him to enter criminal prosecution against me instead, saying *he* would sign such. If the Christian standard of the Presbyterian Church be maintained, of which, at *that* time, this man was an elder, he is a subject for Presbyter *investigation*. And is not *perjury* punishable also in the civil courts? It would not have made the slightest difference to me, at that time; indeed, I really think I would have rejoiced had I been sentenced to hang — to have known that other hands could do for me that which I could not accomplish for myself. Several months later, when I made the attempt at *hanging myself* in my room at the asylum, and Dr. Hester notified my husband, at the same time telling him to be prepared at any time to hear of my death, as I seemed to think of nothing else, he inclosed the doctor's letter to my sister, adding, "As for *me*, I never did take any *stock* in that suicide theory, *nor do I now*" — (an opinion lie still clings to, I believe) — a state of mind, considered by experts among the insane as *hopeless*. Fixed ideas being difficult to combat. By those "outside the bars," the verdict reads mulish. And the mule as an animal has one rare virtue, that of consistency — he kicks, from principle, because its his nature *to* kick, and there's not much else he can do.

CHAPTER IV.

Then, there is no need to speak.
The *universe* shall henceforth speak for you —
And witness — she who did this thing was horn
To do it, claims her *license* in the work,
And so with more works —
— E. B. Browning.

I MUST beg my readers to go back with me to the time when I made the attempt upon my life by taking strychnine. Since I am accused of drawing upon the writings of Victor Hugo for my description of the symptoms of poisoning by strychnine — a piece of great presumption on my part, were it true — my traducers deny the fact of my having taken it at all; ascribing my positive assertions of its truth to my love of notoriety and diseased imagination — therein making a *tacit* acknowledgment of my *insanity*, heretofore *denied*; since, in a diseased mind, the imagination does some times take most wonderful flights. The work referred to of Hugo's — "A Story of a Crime" — I have *yet* in anticipation. Neither do I need the pen of even so ready a writer as he — unsurpassed though he be in vivid pen pictures and in powerful delineation of character — to depict the awful *suffering*, the *horrible agony* of the victim of strychnine poisoning! Victor Hugo, however *realistic* his descriptive powers may be, is but a *theorist*, as are all others who get their information from this or that noted authority of the medical profession, or, possibly, from *observation*. Few know it from experience; and still *fewer* come back from its *terrible death* to attempt to tell its horror.

It has been said, too, as proof of my falsity, that Mr. Kellem, the druggist at Vincennes, denied selling it to me. Well, he is dead; so I can not call him to account, and make him own it. There was *method* in his denial, too, since he was acting in direct violation of the law in selling poison without exercising the *utmost caution.* And he did nothing of the sort, not so much as *asking my name;* though he *did* refuse to sell me more than one dime's worth, when I wished a quarter of a dollar's worth. There is, however, a man in that town—a grocer with whom we had dealings—who, if he will truthfully testify in my behalf, will say that *he* bought an additional dime's worth of it for me; and, putting that with the other, I swallowed it all. The quantity gotten by me seemed so small I was afraid to risk it, as I intended no mistakes should be made that time; and I felt *sure* of *death,* since I was handling poison considered undoubtedly fatal. There are also several intelligent women living in the same town where this occurred, who were present and witnessed my terrible suffering during the half day I was in convulsions—the last one of almost an hour's duration. My last memory, before complete unconsciousness, was of hearing one of my little children saying: "Oh wipe the spit off my mamma's mouth, so I can kiss her!" And I felt the dear little fellow's lips upon mine—and *then* I was at rest!

I wish I had language to describe the lovely scenes that, as visions of a dream, passed before me. Tall waving trees! Lovely undulating hills and valleys, covered with richest verdure and flowers! Sweet singing birds, and babbling, murmuring streams! And then the scene changed, and I seemed to be in some large building, *all alone;* and in the distance, as though *also alone* in some immense empty hall, came indistinctly, but *sweetly,* the sound of *childish voices* in laughter and play. My dream, or vision, whatever it was, was a dim foreshadowing, or premonition, of the hospital ward, upon which I was, in the *new building.* And, after I had been an inmate there *two years*—(the illusion of children's voices was complete, just as distinctly and sweeter, exactly as I heard in my rest, *akin to death!*)—came the voices of Dr. Rogers' little twin boys, echoing and resounding through the halls of the "center building," just outside of our ward. Who can explain this? I simply state the *facts.*

Upon regaining consciousness, I heard first the ticking of the clock; and it seemed to be saying, in a rejoicing tone: "Comeback! Come back!" And I remember saying to a neighbor standing by my bedside: "What a friendly little clock! Do you hear how it is talking to me?" The clock was a wedding present to me from a dear friend, and I often wonder if she ever heard of my dreadful misfortune.

I bought that poison in February of '77, and took it April 21st of the same year. But, in the interval, there was not a day I did not *attempt* to take it, but was withheld from doing so by some sort of power beyond my ken. I seemed always to be *waiting* for some thing! For a time! And at last the time came! I am writing a perfectly truthful account; but my readers must bear in mind, I was an *insane woman* — and they may judge as they see proper of my moral responsibility in the following history.

I was alone that night with my three little ones, with the exception of a servant-girl; and I spent the greater part of the night writing to my husband, trying to tell him how utterly miserable and hopeless I was, and how much better it would be for him and our children since I was so powerless to attend to their comfort — for me to die! And I told him what I anticipated doing. Then I carried my baby — dear little Willie, who has scarcely known a mother's care since his birth! — into the room adjoining, placed him in the bed with his brothers, and kissed them all — as I thought for the *last time*. Then, placing the letter where I knew it would be found when my body was being prepared for the grave, I tried to take the fatal dose! I say I *tried* to take it; for it seemed utterly impossible for me to raise the glass containing it to my lips. I tried to pray, but I could not! Until just as daylight began to glimmer through the closed shutters I, as deliberately and calmly as I ever bargained for the merest trifle, *sold my soul* for permission to die! Some, one, some power, or spirit — call it what you may — was there, in my room, bargaining for my soul;

debating with me as to the price! And, when the compact was sealed, I swallowed the poison!

Now, *why* did I not die? And does that promise still hold good? *Will* my soul be eternally lost? No! A thousand times, no! By my deep humiliation, utter despair, struggles and tears, during those seven dreadful years of insanity, the price is paid! I am redeemed, fearless and content!

CHAPTER V.

> But the goat upon which the lot fell to be scapegoat,
> shall be presented *alive* before the Lord, to make an
> atonement with him, and to let him go for a scape-goat
> into the wilderness. — Leviticus, xiv: 10.

I HAVE always felt a sort of *pity* for that poor "scape-goat" of ancient history, and can more readily sincerely sympathize with him now, since having had a similar experience. The inspired writer failed, however, to follow the fortunes of the poor goat, and we are left to doubt if ever he was permitted to *return to the camp.* Or if, while in the wilderness, any "good Samaritan" gave him a kind word, or proffered assistance in helping him carry his burden, even tho' he could not lighten it. Probably none of these. It's more than likely, since, as he was *originally* a tolerably willful sort of animal, and, as would naturally be the case, not in a very pleasant state of mind at being obliged to shoulder other's sins, including his own small share, by comparison, one may conclude that he was not the most agreeable sort of personage to encounter. So it may be presumed that each person brought in contact with him considered themselves at liberty to improve (?) his temper by sneering looks and insolent commands to "move on!" accompanied by an occasional kick, by way of speeding him on his way. Let us hope the poor fellow was permitted to *kick back*; and if so, he had a sort of satisfaction, after all.

The wilderness into which I was driven by cruel Fate, aided and abetted by heartless brutality within my own immediate household, was the "Asylum for the Insane." Bearing upon my body *suggestive marks*, silent witnesses of *blows*, not given alone by the *tongue*, I envy not that person her peace of mind, if she possesses a conscience, who by her *insulting taunts* and vile insinuations, continued and *persisted in* for three days before I, in my desperation, was *driven* to the act for which I am called an "homicide", a person, too, to whom I had never shown aught but kindness, to whom *often* I had extended generous hospitality, when my home was a pleasant place to come to.

My first night spent at the asylum was a dreadful one to me, although my attendants were very considerate to me. I was placed in a sleeping room in the receiving ward together with *three other* patients, and immediately asked permission of Dr. Hester to sleep in a room by myself, since I was *afraid of insane people*. This request he refused, assuring me that I had no more reason to be afraid of *those other three insane women* than *they* had to be *afraid of me*, a fact I certainly had not thought of before. But this was said kindly, and at bed-time he came in with the "night watch," explaining her duties, and telling me the use of her little lantern, saying she would look in upon me frequently during the night, and I must not be frightened as she flashed her light into my face to see if I were sleeping. From that night I have loved *that* "night watch," and during the few months she remained there afterwards, she was a "friend indeed," as are all who are friends "*in need*," and we are still friends, and often since my recovery, have talked over the sad hours of my affliction; and the ladies who have at different times since filled this responsible position during my stay there, deserve *unstinted* praise for the punctual, watchful discharge of their lonely and sometimes *fearful* duties; for in the "silent midnight watches" these young girls are sometimes called upon to witness death in its most fearful form — self-inflicted! And to me, in my years of almost entire sleeplessness, they seemed, by the glancing light of their lanterns, as they flitted along with almost noiseless step, like "guardian spirits." I don't know that they even *dreamed* I loved them, even when I appeared to be the *incarnation* of *hatefulness*. I am glad of the opportunity of speaking thus publicly of their faithfulness to the trust placed in them.

Before I had been an inmate of the asylum a week I felt a greater degree of contentment than I had felt for a year previous. Not that I was reconciled to life, but because my unhappy condition of mind was understood, and I was treated accordingly. Besides, I was surrounded by others in like *bewildered*, discontented mental state, in whose miseries, each believing their own individual woe the greater, I found myself becoming interested, my sympathies becoming aroused.

I had always loved books, but, strangely enough, had never read any thing of *insanity*, had never thought but little about it; hence these *insane people* were a study — an interesting study, too. And at the same time, I *too*, was treated as an insane woman, a kindness hitherto not shown me, Dr. Hester being the first person *kind enough* to say to me, in answer to my question, "Am I insane?" "*Yes, madam, and very insane*, too! so much so that I very greatly doubt your recovery; and I must say further, that had not the mistaken kindness of your friends kept you *out of this place* almost three years, you might *now* be at home, a well woman, with your children. But," he continued, "we intend to benefit you all we can, and our particular hope, for you. is the restraint of this place." The insane have *no better* friend than Dr. Hester. I heard him once, in reprimanding a negligent attendant, give utterance to this noble sentiment: "I stand pledged to the State of Indiana to protect these unfortunates. I am the *father, son, brother,* and *husband* of over three hundred women! — a tolerably big contract — but I have *undertaken* it, and *I'll see* that they are well taken care of!" I was under his care *nine months*, and he was *unfailing* in his kindness and respectful treatment towards me.

I had not been there long until I noticed that certain patients in each ward were requested, or rather *expected* to go to religious services held in the chapel, and it caused very anxious thought on my part. I was not inclined *then* to disobey any of the rules, but most certainly did not *intend* to *go to church*. So, I asked Dr.

Hester if I would ever be *compelled* to go? "No," he said, "certainly *not*; you are unsettled enough *now* on points of theology. *I* will never force your inclination in that direction; neither do I think any party succeeding us will do so. But I certainly *hope some time* the Lord may so incline your heart that you will go willingly." I don't know at all if the doctor is himself *piously inclined* or not, but as I answered, "Oh, the Lord has nothing at all to do with me! *we* have parted company long since!" he said, "So *you* are able to live independently of the Lord, are you? Well, that's something *I* don't care to try."

This subject of restraint as a *curative* in the treatment of the insane, was again brought before me in a conversation with our superintendent, Dr. Orpheus Everts, a gentleman of superior attainments and experience, and in whom centered all the virtues constituting the true philanthropist. I was one day standing, as I frequently did, at the window, sunken in the deepest melancholy, gazing at I know not what, when I was aroused by his voice asking, "Are you drinking in the beauties of nature?" And truly, the view from that point was lovely! But I answered, "I am not thinking at all whether the sun is shining or clouded; but I remember when I delighted in the loveliness of nature." "And you will again," he said. "Surely as the sun comes from behind the cloud, just *so surely* will you come 'from under the cloud' now enveloping you." I thought differently, and said, "Upon what grounds do you base your hope for me?" "Principally, I think, upon the restraint you are under in this place." "Restraint?" I said, "I am under no restraint," supposing he referred to the numerous mechanical and other restraints in use then (since abolished entirely) in the asylum. And he answered, "*Are you not?*' Look at that window. Could you break one of those bars? See those locked doors? For the first time, probably, in your life, your will is brought directly in opposition to stronger wills. Refuse to go into the dining room at the ringing of the

24

bell, since you are not hungry, or do not *care* to eat. Strong arms will carry you to the table and compel you to swallow food! Say you can not sleep, *therefore will not* go to bed! *You will go!* And if need be, you will be strapped upon the bed, and the key turned against you. *Are* you *not* restrained? Indeed, to one of your temperament, I should imagine you are under fearful restraint." I am not sure if the doctor anticipated such would be the result, but at any rate, from *that moment* I began *resisting* every thing in the slightest approaching *coercion*. But I can truthfully say that there never was a time, subsequent, when I would not have obeyed a *polite request*. But, unfortunately, politeness is a virtue made conspicuous by its scarcity, among attendants upon the insane, as many an *indignant* woman can testify. Generally they are of a class who use their "brief authority" to outrage and humiliate, in every possible manner, the persons so unfortunate as to be in their power. Certainly the position of an attendant upon the insane is not an *agreeable* one — at times it is extremely unpleasant — but it is not compulsory upon *these parties* to remain. There are other positions they might fill more *acceptably*. Kitchens, from which most of them *came*, call loudly for their *return* to more suitable employment. It *does* give them, though, a certain sort of standing among themselves. And I assure you they are quite an "exclusive set" among themselves, drawing the line severely *against* other *outside employes*, often more worthy, and always *more refined*, since *they* have the advantage of associating with ladies, even if it be in the capacity of servants. They have a *dangerous* power, too, and *use* it, without stint, when they can do so without danger of being "reported." Oh, they are a vastly superior party of young ladies, I assure you; and I once heard one of them, considered for several years one of the most "trusty attendants" in the house, say to a lady, after having compelled her to wash half a dozen pairs of stockings for her, "*You* don't *dare* to put on any of your airs with me. I'm *boss* here (a favorite expression among the fraternity), and the State pays me eighteen dollars a month for *making* just such high-toned ladies as you *wash* for me!" To their credit, be it said, there are honorable exceptions among them, and I was fortunate enough to be under the care of two most excellent girls, and I recall many acts of kindness that I bear in grateful remembrance. And it were well for attendants and *others* to bear in mind that kindness *pays*, even among the insane. I remember every single kind word or act, from the beginning, and I remember, and *resent yet*, bitterly, every single *cruelty*. One circumstance bearing upon this point I will relate. Both of my usual attendants were to be absent upon a certain occasion, until midnight, and a "detail" from another ward was appointed to take charge of us. At that time, and for some months previous, I had been wearing "restraints" at night, to prevent a *repetition* of an attempt to hang myself. The "restraints" consisted of leather "*wristlets*," through which was passed a belt crossing the hands and buckling around the waist. Before Miss P—left the ward, she came to me and said, "Now, Mrs. Agnew, I want you to promise me you won't give any body any trouble about your 'restraints' to-night. Let them be put on quietly." And I promised I would. This matter of putting me *upon my honor* as to my *promise*, always prevailed, even in my craziest moments; but, unfortunately, few cared to treat me so respectfully. When these "restraints" were considered necessary, in order that my valuable (?) life be saved, Dr. Hester ordered that they be arranged as comfortable as consistent with safety, and the girls were particular to observe his directions. When bed-time came, the "detail" put all the other patients to bed, and left the ward for a short time, returning with *four* great, strong girls from the back wards, and they came into my room, a mighty, mutual, protection squad, to *assist* in restraining a *dangerous* patient! and in spite of my tearful protestations that *no force* was necessary, threw me upon the bed and drew my strap so tightly as almost to stop my breathing, and the "wristlets" almost cut into my arms; and they left me in that condition until Miss P— — —returned, at midnight. As she was passing my door I called her, and quickly relieving me, she said, as she looked at my poor, swollen hands. "What damned fool did this?" And I said, "Oh, there were *five* of them. It took that many to *protect themselves* against one helpless woman!" I never heard Miss P— — — swear before that time, but I'm sure I didn't think her any less the lady for swearing on that occasion. Do you?

CHAPTER VI.

A child was among them takin' notes,
And faith he'll print 'em. — Burns.

Shortly after the occurrences of the previous chapter it began
to be whispered through the wards of an approaching change
in the administration — the present parties having had charge
of the institution for probably fourteen years. And from
occasional newspapers, that found their way into the hands of
some of the more intelligent patients, we learned that an
investigation (?) was going on, in which our beloved
physicians were charged with all sorts of cruelties and
outrages upon their patients, and I can not properly describe
the indignation it excited among those powerless to testify to
the entire falsity of the charges. Authorities would find
ofttimes that the testimony of this class, who are debarred
from even a *voice* in matters of importance, would be
invaluable in their interests, and quite, if not more reliable,
than those allowed to testify under oath. And in this case had
the patients (certainly the most interested parties) been
allowed to vote, I'm thinking; the verdict would have been
different. What a shame! what cruelty! that politics is
permitted to lay its blighting hand upon this the noblest of
state charities, "The Hospital for Insane!" But so it *was*. One
political power must step down and out "*nolens volens*" that
the victorious other political party walk in with becoming
dignity.

Persons having had no experience among the insane can form
no idea what "change of administration" means to the
inmates, who very soon become entirely conversant with the
details of hospital machinery, and who, as a class, are strong
in their likes and dislikes, and do not readily adopt new ideas
or objects, and persons generally would be surprised, if not
chagrined, could they hear the sarcastic comments and

criticisms and the nice points of comparison drawn by persons who "have lost their minds."

As the officers of the new administration made their first appearance *in the wards* one old lady, who had been a patient for twenty years, therefore witnessing several such changes, and by virtue of *staying* considered herself "one of the family," said with a contemptuous look as one of the new comers was making his first official "round:" "Damned *upstart*, he had better get one of us to show him how to run this *she-bang!*" Everybody in the asylum knew "Aunt Betty" and her tongue, and it was considered the part of wisdom not to question her *right* to remarks, neither was it always safe to reply to them. But she was a reasonable old lady, and, like many of her sane sisters, a little politic, too. So she was not long in recognizing the worthiness of the new administration. Possibly I should offer an apology for the quite frequent use of expletives more *emphatic* than elegant on the score of their profanity. But to be perfectly truthful I can not omit them. There is with scarcely a single exception a profane stage, a downright swearing period! The most refined, delicately brought-up woman will swear at times in a manner perfectly shocking to sensitive ear, and the more religiously inclined the person has formerly been, the more profanely she will swear. And for a complete conglomeration of heterogeneous, theological doctrines commend me to the insane asylum. When this period arrives in certain types of insanity, particularly that of deep seated melancholy, the observant physician hails it as an encouraging symptom. Considers it the climax, or rather the turning point of the malady, and curses loud or deep heaped upon everybody and anybody, often himself included, does *not* shock him. Better this expression of feeling than moody silence. And what an exquisite relief it is to pent-up feeling! What a safety valve to boiling rage at *one's self* and all the world so miserably unconscious of the victim's mental torture! I know when the time came, after years of self debasemement, self condemnation, when I could not so much as lift a finger or an indignant glance to show my deep resentment of outraged feeling! when the time came when I could turn upon my tormentors, friends or foes, with a threatening gesture and an *emphatic* "Go to hell! *God damn* you!" my recovery was a matter of *hope* at least.

And another marked characteristic of the insane is the *seeming, unjustifiable* hatred of those of their friends, formerly and *naturally* the "nearest and dearest." And happy indeed are those of these unfortunates having friends loyal and sufficiently noble *not* to hold them responsible for *insane ravings.* In this as well as other wise (?) arrangements of Providence we see mysteries that we must not question. Among insane men each one is calling down vengeance upon some particular woman, that woman *generally* his wife, *not* always. Among the insane woman, who are generally married women, *the man* upon whom she calls down the especial anathema of heaven is without a single exception *her husband.* And woman-like (Oh the weakness of womankind!) the moment reason returns to its normal condition, that *poor* man! how she *does* long to see him! Don't she *know*, poor fellow, how he is grieved over her absence! And don't she *know* how gladly he will welcome her home! And ofttimes these husbands of sadly afflicted wives and mothers do *grieve for them,* and gladly, *tearfully* welcome them home after weary exile. And there are *others* to whom *home* must be forever *but* a *memory.* I have witnessed some touching meetings between these happily reunited husbands and wives — meetings that seemed necessary to strengthen my unbelieving heart as to the constancy of any man's affection.

No, we must not question the dealings of Providence. We must wait patiently, with unquestioning, childish faith! Must groan even unto fainting under burdens *too* heavy for poor humanity, until —

> "In the hereafter angels *may*
> Roll the stone from the grave *away*"

And we will know *why*. I prefer a surer compensation and a speedier. And why *not* question? Children get old enough to question their earthly parentage, and to demand answers, too. And have they not the right? Why not also question our heavenly Father? But this is a digression, and it is better that I should not disturb settled points of theology. It is probably best I should let these doubtful matters *alone*, severely even, tho' my heart be stinging and aching over their *injustice* since my ideas are not popular.

In October, '79, the state having completed a magnificent new hospital for the exclusive use of the women, we were removed from our old quarters into the new, standing within the same grounds, and but a short distance. To a sympathetic beholder some of the scenes of that flitting were touching in the extreme! The home instinct, I think, largely predominates in women. And there were few exceptions among the more intelligent patients who did not regret leaving the old house in anticipation of handsome quarters in the new building. Many had to be forced by main strength to leave, since they had gotten the idea that they were to be taken to the penitentiary — for, I assure you, there are scores of self-convicted criminals in all such institutions who suffer untold torture from the fear of arrest for some fancied crime. Others wept and implored permission to *stay* just simply because they did not want to go! They didn't want to *do* any thing! Oh, dear! They *only* wanted to be *left alone*! *Exactly* so! And a few years later, when a part of this beautiful edifice was wrapped in flames and the whole house greatly in danger of burning, this same helpDless, listless inactive class of patients, would have perished rather than use the slightest exertion to get out of danger. Oh! the simple horror of this dreadful something that gets possession of one's faculties to such a degree as to utterly paralyze even the instinct of self-preservation — nature's first law!

CHAPTER VII.

"Who never mourned hath never known
What treasures grief reveals,
The sympathies that humanize
The tenderness that heals." — W. H. Burleigh.

Soon after my admission I formed the acquaintance of a woman of unusual intelligence, an inmate of an adjoining ward, whom I frequently met when out walking for exercise. We had many thoughts in common and congenial literary taste, but directly opposite in our ideas regarding the sinfulness of *suicide*. I openly expressed my sincere belief that since we were brought into the world independent of our wish or will, we had a perfect right to chose whether or no we stay here, after life hath lost its charms, and was to us simply an impatiently borne burden! We had one last talk together the day upon which the new building was given over into the hands of the state trustees, and the crowds of people and band of music, attendant upon the occasion, seemed to worry her dreadfully. As usual, in our conversations, we talked of suicide, together with the question of the possible return of departed spirits and their communication with their friends. During our conversation she said: "Well, my friend, you and I have had pleasant, enjoyable times together here, but I must believe that suicide is the unpardonable sin! since for *this* there is no repentance. So, if I should kill myself to-night, I believe I should go *right straight to hell!* I don't presume in that case I would be permitted to return, neither do I suppose you would care to receive a visit from a *lost soul*! And should I be so unspeakably happy as to find myself in heaven I might not be inclined to leave there, even for a short time. But just as surely as spirits are permitted to return, when I go *away*, I will *return to you!*" As we parted in the hall separating our wards, she said good-by! *I* shall not go over to the new house. She was not a patient requiring close attention during the night, and in the morning her dead body was found suspended *stiff* and *stark* in her lonely little room! And her soul, pure and white, I am certain, had found the mystery of all its sad questionings. Did she return to me? Time and again! Not with the stooping, fragile body and care-stamped face of my departed friend! but with the springing, buoyant step, and bright laughing face of her early married life, so often talked of when she counted not past years by their tears and dreamed of no hereafter without its joyous hopes. Explain this if you can. My belief is that she is to-day *loving again* in some bright *happy* child! I am not a believor in any form of spiritualism that I have ever read of or heard spoken of, but I have a theory that insane persons are brought directly under spiritual influence *not* to be explained. My father was with me constantly for months! So sensible was I of his presence that I often put out my hand, thinking *surely* I would touch him. But the time came when he said, "I am going to leave you now, my daughter, and I am *not* coming back again!" And from that time I was *indeed alone*!

Shortly- after our removal to the new house I had a so-called "period of excitement" — that of raving insanity. I was conscious of my inability to control myself! Knew I was screaming, laughing and praying without the power to stop. And through it all, right into my poor dazed brain, rang this sentence, constantly repeated in a horribly mocking tone; "By every art known to scientific druggists shall thy body be tortured and thy *soul tormented* by a secret known only to the Jews." From whence came this warning? — for warning it certainly was. I can not answer but I do know the promises or threatened torment, and consequent torture, followed speedily. The "secret," I yet believe, meant masonry. And during the remaining years of my insanity some of my most pronounced and peculiar "delusions" were connected with that order, of which my father was for many years an honored member, and at that time *I* was a mason's wife!

"Oh, Christ I that it were possible
For one short hour to see,
The souls of those we love that they might tell us
What and *where* they be" — Tennyson

CHAPTER VIII.

Oh life! thou art a galling load
Along a rough and weary road,
To wretches such as I. — Burns.

How gladly I would pass silently over the incidents of the
three following years. I hesitate to put upon record the events
of those years of mental darkness, degradation and despair.
Even now my nights are rendered sleepless at the review of
them. When by the resurrecting eye of memory these ghosts of
my sad past go flitting by, I shiver and grow cold at the
recollection of the depths into which I was driven. Even self-
respect, that last hope of womanhood, almost extinguished —
every single sin of the decologue was involuntarily assumed,
and I felt the consequent condemnation *more keenly*, I
presume, than would have been the case had I in reality been
guilty of their violation. I had been an inmate of the asylum
about nine months, and was standing one morning, as I
frequently did, at the window, wishing, oh, so anxiously, for a
newspaper. It was noticed by this time that I seemed to derive
more pleasure from reading, particularly the daily papers,
than from any thing else, hence, I was deprived of this slight
comfort. Had they known that my special craving for the daily
news was to gratify a morbid curiosity that I had to know how
far my *infernal* influence extended, which influence, I believe
to be the direct cause of the numerous murders, suicides, and
various other outrages, together with all sorts of calamities of
land and water, mind and nerve, not excepting an occasional
earthquake, they might have refused me the papers upon the
grounds of kindness to refuse to encourage such morbid
"delusions." But I was yet sufficiently master of myself *not* to
betray these thoughts, and I am compelled to the belief that it
was the beginning of a system of persecution, perfectly
outrageous and sinful, for a period of several years. I

remember wondering, as I stood there, if my friends at home could know that I more earnestly wished for a newspaper than I ever craved food, if they would not pity me, and the thought occurred to me to write to my — just at this moment our supervisoress touched my arm and said, "Come with me, Mrs. Agnew." and walking down the hall to my room, opened the door, and there stood my husband. I think, for a moment or so, I never was so happy. It was his first visit to me. And only a moment ago I was feeling so utterly wretched and alone. But now my husband had come, and he did care something for me after all. After I had entered the room, and closed the door, he stood looking at me, but not speaking a word until I said, "For heaven's sake, don't stand there staring at me in such a manner as that; sit down and say something to me; ask me something, or I shall *scream* through sheer nervousness." So he took the chair I offered him, drew it closely up to mine, and gazing into my eyes, said: "Were you insane when you were *married*?" Not one single, little word of kindness or gesture of tenderness, not the shadow of a greeting; simply this cruel, *calculating* question. Evidently, he had *even then* formed the determination that I should never leave that asylum alive. I did not then think this, however, and answered, most assuredly, "I was *not* insane when we were married." I have changed my opinion since then, materially, and willingly admit I *was insane*, and my most pronounced symptom was that I *married him*. After a time I said, "Have you nothing to say to me? Can't you tell me something of my children?" "*Your* children!" he replied. "Why, I hadn't an idea you *cared* to hear from them. You don't certainly presume to profess to love them?" Oh, it was inhuman, to so torture a poor, helpless woman; yet I doubt if in his egotism he realized my suffering. He asked if I wished to see my children, and I said, "No, I did not *dare* to see them," and this, I presume, was additional proof to his charitable (?) soul, of my hatred of my children, and he said, "Very well; I will never *bring* those children to see you until you ask me to."

After obtaining permission from the physician in charge, he took me out walking, and while there, my outraged feelings got the better of my pride, and I charged him with having lost all regard or affection for me, and he answered, "Oh, no, Anna, you are quite mistaken; I love you just as well as I ever did;" and then followed rapid questions, to which he *demanded* answers that proved the nature of his regard for me, past and present, and from that moment my faith in his purity was a thing of the past. Another "delusion" gotten clear of. Tennyson knew whereof he spoke when he penned the following:

> What is this? his eyes are heavy; think not they are glazed with wine.
> Go to him, it is thy duty; kiss him, take his hand in thine;
> It *may* be my lord is weary, that his brain is overwrought;
> Soothe him with thy finer fancies, touch him with thy lighter thought
> He will answer *to the purpose*, easy things to understand.
> Better thou wert dead before him, though he slew thee with his hand.

In a letter written since by him, filled with abuse and misstatements of me, he considers it necessary to conclude with the following superfluous, high-flown sentiment — superfluous since he *innately* has not the *slightest conception* of the sanctity of that relation: "But, after *all* (all what)? I *must remember* that she is the mother of my children." I have long since relieved him from the necessity of making the effort to remember that fact.

My readers will understand that my despondency was constantly deepening, and my "delusions" becoming daily more fixed and distressing, though possibly, to those around me, I appeared much the same. Scarcely a single exception is observed among the insane of freedom from so styled "delusions," and the unfortunate victims are as confident of entire freedom from them, as they are ready to recognize their *presence* in their neighbor, and it is laughable, sometimes, and at the same time piteous, to listen to their crazy criticisms of each other. I asked a lady one day whose mother was also insane, and who had formerly been in the same ward with her daughter, *where* her *mother* was, and she answered, "Oh, *we* had to send her to a *back ward*, she was so awfully crazy." We had to! And *she* was more insane than her mother had ever been, but was in blissful unconsciousness of the fact; and it is a positive blessing *to be thus unconscious*. Some of these persons are perfectly happy in their "delusions," but such are *generally* hopelessly insane. I believe the patients, generally, liked me, at any rate, I was made the recipient of many a tale of woe, and petitioned for sympathy, at the same time feeling myself the whole cause of all the misery surrounding me. Call this morbid nonsense, pretentious ignorance if you please; to me it was painfully real, and I used to wonder *why* those poor wretches did not realize *what I was*, did not recognize my fearful influence, and rid the world of such a monster by tearing me limb from limb. So deeply did I feel that I was set apart as the "evil one" that I felt compelled to write to my sister to this effect, and in the letter shown me after my recovery, I read this terrible renunciation: "I *have* no mother, brothers, sisters, husband, nor children! I must stand *alone*, now and forever! And as my pen leaves that word *forever*, I claim it as mine. No one else has a right to use it. It is mine, since I, of all humanity understand its complete meaning, its fearful significance! The struggle is between the Almighty and myself, and will last *forever!* I am under the horrid wheel, almost crushed! *Not quite!* The Hand has me in its powerful grasp, but I can still struggle, and I WILL!" The wheel and the Hand had reference to a tormenting repeated dream that in my childhood haunted me, making my nights fearful. Let me try and recall this dream. In the distance would appear a wheel not larger than a silver dollar, which revolving rapidly, growing larger at each revolution, until its dimensions were monstrous when it reached me, would seem about to crush me to atoms, but just at this point some power would stop it, and it would grind and grind with a horrible noise, as tho' angry that its vengeance was stayed, and slowly it would roll backward. Again, a hand, seemingly not larger than an infant's, would appear in the space above, growing larger and fearfully strong as it approached with outstretched fingers as tho' to clutch me, poor, frightened child, by the throat, and I would awaken shivering with fear, and would pray that such terrible things be not sent me. I had a *child's faith* then, and believed that which we prayed for would be granted unto us, because *He said so!* This determined I *will!* And I will *not!* adhered to through the succeeding years of torture, mental and physical; this unbending resolution *not* to be trampled into the dirt, even though I be in the deepest sloughs of insanity; the stinging sense of the injustice of the *undeserved* contempt with which I was treated, made me solemnly swear that *sometime* I would make my persecutors feel the strength of the womanhood within me, however deeply it was then sunken! "I will *break* that woman's devilish *will* or I will break her *damned neck!*" were the words spoken in my hearing by the physician in charge of our ward. *Not* by our superintendent, a thousand times *no!* I am positive now that Dr. Rogers was in entire ignorance of the shameful abuse to which I was subjected by that man who *died* trying to supersede him, but I *dared* not complain even to *him*. Indeed, at that time I was so utterly wretched that I doubted if complaint *from me* would have been listened to even by our superintendent — a cultured scholar and gentleman who bad formerly offered me very respectful attention. I had gained the ill will of his assistant, the physician above-mentioned, and it was necessary for his reputation, in that institution, that I did not put *into words* my knowledge of his utter unworthiness of the position he occupied, and he ordered me transferred from the pleasant, cheerful ward upon which I had been since our removal from the "other house," into a ward occupied exclusively by *epileptics* — a class of patients of whom I stood in dreadful fear — hoping by such treatment that I would be so terrified as to become in *reality* the *imbecile*, that he wrote to my sister, he was *pained to say* I was fast becoming. I was transferred to that ward on the 20th of May, 1880, and walked back into my *former ward* about the same date, one year after, with the same old calico dress hanging in tatters upon me, unchanged and unwashed, and with the same class of undergarments, changed each week for cleanliness, but the *quality* or character *not increased* during the bitter cold winter of '80 and '81, and my greeting from the young lady (?) in charge of the ward (one of the *exclusives*) upon my return was: "Hello! here comes the *devil* back!" My readers will please bear in mind that this treatment was in direct accordance with the physician's *orders* concerning *me*. "*Don't* give that woman a change of *dress* until she *asks* for it," were his words, and I presume I would have worn that blessed calico frock until it dropped thread by thread off me, since I came of stubborn old English stock on *one side* and *Dutch* on the other, only that I was weak enough in bodily strength one day to fall helpless in a congestive chill, in which condition I was for an hour before I was allowed to be put to bed, since, as the "young lady" said, when told by the doctor, after he had examined me, that "I was a very sick woman, and *should* have been in bed *long before*." "Well, I couldn't tell whether she was really sick or just *acting up!*" In consequence of this I was confined to my bed, pretty sick, too, for several weeks, and upon being taken up and ordered to dress myself in a complete *new outfit*, consisting of comfortable clothing, that all the preceding winter, while I was shivering with cold, had been stored away in the "clothing room," my indignation got the better of my small stock of prudence, and I was suddenly possessed of a "destructive spell," and, tho' so weakened by sickness as not to be able scarcely to *stand alone*, I had sufficient strength to tear into hits four dresses as they were given me in succession, for which I was punished by having my arms *twisted* by two strong attendants, discipline considered necessary to *subdue* an *"unruly patient."* Before the *"fight"* was over the breakfast bell rang and I was driven into the dining-room, clad in a *single garment*, with the exception of my shoes and stockings, and was seen in this condition by the engineer, who came in before we were dismissed from the dining-room, to attend to some necessary repairs. The morning succeeding my transfer to the epileptic ward, the physician spoken of, in making his morning "round," seated himself at a table just as I was in the act of placing a glass from which I had been drinking, on the table, and looking up at me, said in a tantalizing tone of mock respect: *"Good* morning, Mrs. Agnew!" I took no notice of his salutation, but walked on toward my chair, when he sprang to his feet, with eyes flashing, and face white with anger, and said: "Don't you *dare* treat *me* with such contempt! *Speak* to me, madame!" and I, folding my arms, walked up to within *striking* distance, and said: "You go to hell, sir!" I hope he was *satisfied* with my *speaking*, and I trust my readers will consider that I was an insane woman at the time, under *his* supposed *protection*, and that the day previous he had *grossly insulted* me, the nature of which insult I will not soil this fair page in attempting to describe.

> Give me an ounce of civit, good apothecary,
> To sweeten my imagination. —Shakespeare.

CHAPTER IX.

When sorrows come, they come not single spies,
But in battalions;
One woe doth tread upon another's heels,
So fast they follow. — Shakespeare.

During my year upon the epileptic ward, I have not one word
to say of my treatment by the attendants. They were as kind to
me as they dared to be, and as I would allow them to be; and I
frequently heard them commenting severely upon the
unkindness of my being kept among such a class of patients. I
soon learned though, that however frightful my surroundings
had been there — to which I never could have become
accustomed, and whose horrible sights and sounds had
completely wrecked my nervous system — there were greater
trials in store for me. On my return from my year's
punishment, the attendants whom I left in this ward were
gone and their places supplied by girls, "after the physician's
own heart." This ward was one of eight visiting wards, open
from 10 A. M. until 5 P. M., to any and every body who felt
disposed to lounge through them, staring at the helpless
inmates, and wondering and disappointed if they were not
treated to some "crazy" manifestation over which they could
laugh for days after. Directly back of these wards, was a tier of
wards not open to the casual visitor, and I would have
considered myself supremely blessed, by comparison, had
they put me on one of those, but no such mercy was intended.
In each ward there are generally one or more unfortunates to
whom the attention of visitors is directed in particular, on
account of some peculiarity of "delusion," sometimes quite
amusing, such as our "Mrs. President Arthur," "Mrs. Gov.
Wood," "Mrs. President Hayes," and an occasional "Queen
Victoria." But of all the monstrosities in this immense
"museum," I was the superlative one. Of course every body

and their "uncles, and aunts, and cousins" would embrace the opportunity of seeing the devil! particularly so, since they could have a view of the Satanic majesty at a moderately short range, when attended by a body-guard, consisting of one usher and two attendants who felt the "contempt that familiarity breeds," and as a consequence, were not afraid of the devil. Oh! I assure you, kind reader, I was a wretch of marked distinction and prominence; and in order to further mortify the little remaining self-respect, I was not compelled, as were the other patients, to change my clothing; so rage and dirt added attraction to my already miserable appearance. At that time the doors of our sleeping rooms were locked as soon as the beds were made in the morning, and remained so until the "retiring bell" rang; so the poor comfort of hiding my misery within the friendly shelter of my own room was denied me, and there I sat in the "devil's corner," so designated and known all over the house for nearly two years, motionless almost, and speechless, excepting an occasional muttered oath, or threatening gesture at the too near approach of friend or foe. I recognized no difference and resented almost as keenly, the tears of former friends, dropped occasionally upon my face as they silently stood beside me, as I did the brutal command of my attendants to "Get right straight up there, and walk yourself into that dining-room, madam, or I'll drag you there!" Every single command accompanied by a threat—a proceeding not particularly soothing to a sane person of any spirit, and particularly exasperating to an insane one, who, when at herself, would have considered her tormentors beneath contempt. The greater part of the time I was too deeply sunken in desperate thought to hear the bell when it rang, but just as surely as the threat was made of dragging me in, it had to be executed, as often by my hair as by my arms, and after having dragged me into the room and compelled me to swallow food, they were obliged to drag me out again; I don't remember ever to have walked out after such performance.

One subject I feel it is my duty, for the sake of like sufferers, to speak freely of, even at the risk of offending sensitive, fastidious readers. I must enter my most emphatic protest against patients being compelled to eat, and particularly of being held and forcibly made to swallow food. Certainly if I could make the humane physician understand that even now I am made deathly sick at the mere recollection of my horribly disgusting "delusions" regarding the nature of the food I was compelled to swallow for weeks together, they would, without a single exception, strike that clause from their "ward rules." Think of it for a moment: at times I would feel fearfully hungry, but the moment I was seated at the table, every single article would become alive, creeping, squirming vermin of all disgusting characters was in the food put upon my plate; and when, as was natural, I could not put those vile things into my mouth, an attendant would hold my hands behind me, and another pour liquids down my throat, choking me so I must swallow or strangle *human filth*. Raw eggs, without a suspicion of salt, pepper or any thing else to make them in the least palatable, were freely choked into my rebellious stomach; and the reality of my dreadful "delusion" would not be more disgusting to me now than it was then. But I was helpless, and so are thousands of other poor women. Under that man's reign I have seen those heartless girls fill a quart cup with a mixture of all the vegetables on the table, then salt and pepper and mustard by the spoonful, and after filling up the cup with vinegar, stir up the nasty mess, and feed it by tablespoonsful to some miserable wretch, crowding it down the unwilling throat—at the same time taunting and giggling over their misery—all this to teach them to "eat decently, like other folks." I pity the lowest wretch that ever fell into their clutches.

My readers may naturally infer that there were some grounds for me being considered the "most troublesome patient in the institution." But, at the same time, a polite request to go into the dining-room, or a simple notification that the bell was ringing, would have been obeyed quietly, if not gracefully. There is not that person lives who has not something of the devil. It is a universal inheritance; and it is not at all surprising that woman, more readily than man, succumbs to the satanic influence, since she it was who first formed the acquaintance of his majesty.

Sometime previous to these occurrences, in a "crazy spell," I had felt compelled to destroy every scrap of writing, letters and such, bearing upon them my name — even going so far as to efface my name written by my husband upon the back of my children's photograph. I had a morbid dread of hearing or seeing my name; and this, too, was taken advantage of; and as a consequence my name was rung into my ears, by constant useless repetition, until I had a positive hatred for its very sound, and I was so nearly wild with anger that murder was not a strange thought, had I found the opportunity. At three different times, too, I took off my wedding-ring and threw it away; but, as soon as the paroxysm passed, I asked for its return. It seemed, at such times, I could not bear it upon my hand, and for days together I could locate a small burning spot upon my finger, made, it seemed to me, by the date and inscription within it. Was not that a premonition of what the future held — a dissolution of the tie between us, of which that ring was the emblem? At last, one day, I asked one of the patients, who was very kind to me, to take it off, and never let me see it again. But it was kept safely for me, and I again put it on, writing on a little note book — "February 23, 1883; I will wear this ring, spite of hell!" and I am wearing it yet. As a consequence of sitting so constantly, and disregarding nature's demands, least, in taking the few steps necessary to reach the closet, some taunt be flung at me, my health became completely shattered, and I had scarcely strength sufficient to walk the length of the hall.

I spoke several chapters back of having some very peculiar delusions regarding Masonry. Let me tell you how I suffered in consequence of them. One of the rules of the ward was that each patient, able to do so, should make her own bed, and at night take off the spread and fold it in a particular manner, which, when so folded, presented to my disturbed mind the appearance of a large book; and it was white. My ruling spirit (what was it?) solemnly commanded me, in the name and the fear of Masonry, not to touch that great white book, and, had my life have been the forfeit, I would not have disobeyed that voice, I had not the strength to make my bed, and at night, when going to bed, had persistently disregarded my attendant's orders to fold my spread, or even to remove it. Upon one occasion, one of my attendants being away on a "furlough," and the other one not being able for active duty, there were two girls detailed from one of the back wards for several days' duty on ours. At supper-time I heard my attendant say to the details: "You two girls are used to devils on your ward, so I want you to make 'Old Agnew' (omitting the Mrs.) fold her spread tonight. Just you two break her in while you are in here; I'm too weak, myself, to tackle her, and I don't care if you half kill her, so you don't leave any marks where Mrs. Rogers can see, or she will tell the doctor, and then the devil will be to pay." Mrs. Rogers was the wife of our superintendent, and also matron, and came frequently through the wards. To say that I was terrified does not express my feelings. I knew they did not dare to kill me. Indeed, just then, I would not have cared, if they had. But I knew some fearful abuse was in store for me, and, oh! how helpless and alone I was. I could not fold that spread. I did not dare to. It was white, and I was too vile to touch any thing white. I was afraid to disobey that voice, so I went to bed as usual, leaving the spread upon the bed. After every other patient was securely locked in their room, so that none could come to my assistance, if they even had dared to do so, they both came into my room, and pulling out my little single bed, so that one of them could get behind it, they seized my hands, and began, as usual, to twist my bands, until I screamed with agony, at which they stopped my mouth with the blankets, saying, as they struggled with me: "So you are the high-toned lady who wont mind her attendants, are you? Do you know we are going to choke the life out of you, if you don't get up this minute and fold your spread?" At the same time, dragging me out of bed, they threw me violently on the floor, and knocked my elbows against the hard wood until they were bleeding, leaving stains upon the floor. I was on the bed and on the floor half a dozen times before the "fight" was over, and once, when getting my breath sufficiently, I screamed loudly for Mrs. Rogers. They threw me down upon the bed, both of them getting upon me, while one of them struck me repeatedly with the heel of her shoe upon my head, saying: "You dare to scream again, you infernal old devil, and I'll kill you!" And the other one said: "Don't strike her again, she might tell Dr. or Mrs. Rogers; there's no telling what these damned crazy things will do." And so they left me more dead than alive, fearing to remain longer, least the "nightwatch," on her "first round," would catch them, when, to use their own language, "hell would be to pay," since she would report any such outrage to the superintendent. The morning following I could scarcely move; I could not dress myself, and they helped me up, dressed me, and took me to the dressing-room, where they combed handsful of loosened tangled hair oat of my bruised aching head; then drove me to the dining-room, when the three, as an incentive to appetite, laughed and sneered over the very worst "fight" they ever did have, and talked of an "additional dose" they intended giving me the following night. But, before night, I fainted, and was again in bed for a week. Before that, however, I had been trying to make up my mind to at least show my bruised wrists and bleeding elbows to Mrs. Rogers, but she did not come in, another proof to my morbid mind that she did not care, and had stayed out of the ward purposely; and besides I knew, even then, that, even had it been reported, it was a nice point in hospital etiquette for the superintendent to question the acts of his (the ward physician) in the way of interfering in his authority regarding his patients, and these girls were only instruments in the hands of their superior officer, at the same time were glad of the opportunity of humiliating and at the same time of abusing a lady. From my earliest recollection I have most earnestly protested against the misfortune of being a woman, and since my experience as an insane woman, am less reconciled. I don't believe men are ever so cruel to men. With them it is usually a knock down, with an oath, and that is the end of the matter. They do not, they can not, use their tongues and eyes to cut, and sting, and torture each other as women do, for which, I suppose, we must again blame our curious old "Mother Eve," and, though it is humiliating to think of statistics of insanity proves that both in language and action insane women are worse than their brethren in affliction. I do not remember a single instance of a man, or crowd of men, making an unkind or curious remark concerning my, appearance within my hearing.

CHAPTER. X.

Men, all over this beautiful land of ours, it is your mother, wife, daughter, and sister who are being thus outraged. In every asylum in the land some such scenes are daily enacted, and it will be so, must be, until state laws are so amended as to make such abuses impossible. The willing hands and sympathetic hearts of our noble band of superintendents and their corps of assistant physicians must be encouraged and strengthened by furnishing them experienced nurses, in place of present thoughtless, heartless girls. The establishment of suitable "training schools" will necessarily require time, but, in the meantime, there are hundreds of worthy needy women, widowed mothers, who, having themselves suffered sorrow, have pitying hearts toward their afflicted sisters. Such should speedily replace the others, most of whom consider they are doing the different states honor, since they condescend to accept their money by simply gracing the wards of these asylums for the insane.

Reforms are being instituted all over the land in hospital treatment, and the humane heads of these institutions need only the hearty cooperation of the law-makers to make these hospitals asylums indeed to the unfortunate victims of fate and heritage. In a concluding chapter will be found a letter addressed to the Indiana legislature, which the editor of the *Indianapolis Herald* chooses to call "A Touching Appeal," bearing particularly upon another matter, in which I feel the most profound interest. Let the public make this a personal matter, since there is scarcely a family exempt from this fearfully increasing malady. The bolt may strike some beloved member of your immediate family circle to-day, my friend, with whom I am talking; and lightning strikes twice or thrice, sometimes, in the same household. Ought you not, then, see to it that your loved ones, whom you are compelled to put away from home and you, be withheld from curious gazers by a law prohibiting promiscuous visiting within the wards of our hospitals for the insane?

CHAPTER XI.

Oh, life! thou art a galling load,
Along a rough and weary road,
To mortals such as I. — Burns.

There was a period of almost three years, in which I was almost as completely separated from my former friends as though the silence of the grave were between us. Occasional letters of inquiry were received by the officials, but I was not notified of them. Occasionally, too, a former friend, though oftener, a mere acquaintance, would be granted permission to attempt to interview me, which attempt would be so bitterly and wrathfully resented that few cared to make the second attempt. And at rare intervals some one would come quietly and sit down beside me, and using my old pet name, my little dead brother's best attempt at pronouncing my father's favorite name for me, "daughter," and which all my immediate loved ones called me, would say, "Do you know me, Dottie?" Know them! would I ever forget any one using that dear home name? And though every nerve was tingling at the sound, and my desolate heart actually aching at the thought that right there beside me was one who had loved me, did love me yet, possibly, and would go away sorrowful, because I seemed to have forgotten or cared not to see them, yet I could not speak, could not even raise my eyes, could not silently clasp their hands. I must not give my hand to a friendly grasp — Masonry forbade me that, too. I am not sure how long I entertained this "delusion," something over five years, I think. I remember one day, as I was resting upon the sofa in the ward, after my recovery had become hopeful, though, at the time, I was recovering from a slight sickness, our superintendent came in with some visitors, and saying, kindly, "I am sorry to hear you have been sick," gave me his hand in a natural manner, which I took, without the slightest hesitation. The spell was broken, and he was a Mason. I think, at this time, my misery had about reached its climax. But, before the "turning of the tide," there occurred an outrage, the effects of which will go with me to my grave, if it be not in itself the cause of a lingering, painful death, and I don't care to die now; I have something to hope for in the future. Shortly before this occurrence, one of my attendants, of whom there were two sisters, obtained a position as a "special attendant" upon a lady who was removed from our asylum to her home in Indianapolis. So there was a vacancy in the fourth ward, a very desirable position, too, since it was a front ward, nicely furnished, plenty of flowers, well-drilled servants (washwomen included), among the patients; a fine Steinway piano and a good class of patients, excepting the devil. The choice fell upon a woman upon one of the back wards, a married woman, who frequently quoted, "my husband," since the possession of such an appendage does give a sort of importance to a sort of woman, even though he does not support her. I never saw that woman before she came on the ward, shortly before supper-time. She was received by her future partner with outstretched arms, since all over the house she had the reputation of being "such a sweet woman." And, "Oh! she could play the piano so nicely — my!" At night, when unlocking the sleeping-rooms, as she came to mine, she said to one of the patients sitting near: "Who sleeps here?" And, upon being told it was my room, she opened the door, and deliberately spit a great nasty mess into my room. This was my introduction to Madame C, the pink of perfection. Do you wonder, reader, that I hated her from that moment. I claim only to be human. I don't profess any saintly attributes, and I do claim there's no merit, either in possessing or professing sufficient meekness either to forgive or forget such an uncalled-for insult. It was simply bestial. Even as I write, my indignant blood protests against the effort to forget it. She had had her instructions, I presume, in regard to her treatment of me, and proved herself fully competent to do any dirty bidding, and right well she followed her natural inclination, until, during this last administration, she was delicately (?) hinted out of the institution. And, as she was leaving, I staggered up out of "my corner," and called after her: "Cleaning house on the fourth ward; good riddance of bad rubbish! There's more trash leaving this house this morning than ever left it at one time." She threw a startled, frightened glance over her shoulder, as she sped down the hall, as much surprised, I imagine, as though a dead woman had sat up in her coffin, and hurled those truths at her. Sometimes though, during her palmy days there, I almost forgot her, listening to her music. I loved music passionately, and was tempted sometimes to remind her that expressions in music did not consist of loud pedal, rolled up eyes, or flying fingers. But I am wandering from my point. Shortly after her transfer to our ward, her partner was again prostrated with one of her frequent, hemorrhages of the lungs, and a "detail" was again necessary. One day, while in the dining-room at dinner, I had occasion to leave the room, and had only barely reached the "closet," when the "detail" followed me, and, as usual, ordered me to return to the dining-room. I was not in a condition to return, and sat down on a chair, saying, I could not go back there, and she answered, "Go, this moment, or I'll drag you there;" and she seized me by the arm, and, as I fell, dragged me full length, lying on my back, into the dining-room, the distance being the length of the short hall. Just as she had gotten me across the threshold, Madame C. sprang up, and said: "Don't let her go back to her place at the table; make her lie there, so the 'ladies' (this was the term used to designate the patients, and I detest the sound of it) can walk over her, when they are dismissed from the dining-room. And, 'ladies,'" turning toward their tables, "every single one of you spit on her as you pass out." Spitting seemed her strong weapon of insult, and, in my fearful anger, I attempted to spit on her, a vain attempt, though; for, in times of such angry excitement, there is no saliva secreted — the tongue

54

becomes so parched, and the throat so constricted, that it is almost an impossibility to cry out. But the attempt was sufficient provocation. She sprang upon me, as I lay upon the floor, calling, at the same time, for the "detail" to sit upon my lower limbs, and she pressed both hands, with all her strength, against my head, almost flattening my face against the hard floor, at the same time bearing the weight of her whole body directly upon my chest, one of her knees being planted squarely upon my left breast. When my agony became insupportable, I cried: "Oh! do have mercy; you are crushing my breast." And she answered: "It's a pity about your-." And the name she used does not apply to a woman's breasts. But she got off me, and I struggled to my feet, when they both seized me again, and began the usual torture of twisting my arms; and I can assure the uninitiated that it does not require more than two twists from brutal hands to bring the poor victims to their knees, a devotional attitude, not usually, under such circumstances, attended with, prayer, most frequently with oaths from the victim, and vile, insulting expletives from the young ladies! While struggling with me, trying to make me promise I would "behave myself," something no one ever did succeed in making me promise, since I never began a fight, "our invalid" said: "I'm real sorry, girls, that I'm not able to take a hand in that fight." Then words, plenty of them, came to my assistance, and said: "No, thank God! you are not able to take a hand; your hand has been lifted for the last time against poor insane women. The Lord has laid his hand upon you. You are going to die, do you know it? and that soon." And dying she was, the lingering death of the consumptive; yet, with her gasping breath, could express her regret at her inability to yet give me a blow!

The man, at whose instigation these abuses were heaped upon me, is gone; those two sisters are gone—where? Heaven pity the childish bodies who are now their dwelling-places; and heaven grant that, before their inherited cruelty shall have time to bud and blossom, humanity may have taken such rapid strides as to render their influence harmless.

After the fight was over, which was my last physical "fight," I staggered back to "my corner," in such a wrathful, wicked state of mind as to be absolutely frightful even to recall. After a time, two old ladies came and stood beside me, and talked in a low voice of the outrage, and one of them said: "We two old women should tell Dr. Rogers how this poor creature has been abused. She is dreadfully hurt, for it is a dangerous thing to bruise a woman's breast." But they agreed that they didn't dare "report their attendants," and, as a consequence, no one outside was made acquainted with this "ward secret."

Four years have passed, and I am yet, at times, a fearful sufferer from that painted, smiling fraud's brutality, while she is still not without hope of again receiving employment at the Indiana State Hospital, and her companion in the outrage now occupies the position of attendant at "Anchorage," an asylum in Kentucky, and is as thoroughly an unfeeling and heartless girl as it has ever been my misfortune to meet. Yet it is more than probable her superintendent will read these disclosures doubtfully, since no one knows any better than herself the art of deceiving those in authority.

CHAPTER XII.

I remember with amusement the perfect storm of indignation that was aroused among the attendants when soon after Dr. Fletcher's appointment as superintendent, he abolished "mechanical restraints" of all descriptions. This action of the superintendent, together with the fact of his making a bonfire of the restraints in the presence of the majority of the patients, and accompanied by religious services, singing, prayer, etc., was at the time commented upon in all the Western newspapers, very few commending the wholesale sacrifice, many considering (while they did not directly approve of the system of "restraints,") that the manner of getting clear of the objectionable articles, might have been managed with less of the sensational phase.

But the attendants, what a blow at their dignity! What a curtailment of long established fearfully abused power! How they did splutter. "Only think of it. Not allowed to 'twist arms,' can't even 'camisole.' Why don't you think, the carpenter came in to-day and took out the very last one of our 'restraint chairs.' How ever we are to manage the set in our ward, the Lord only knows. And don't you forget it, every single one of the "nasty things" knew before two days that we did not dare restrain them any more. Oh, its just too bad." I believe it is generally conceded that the change was a beneficial one, both to patients and conscientious attendants. The wards are sweeter — as to atmosphere — and pleasanter to the sight. Since the majority of "restraints" are suggestive of possible outrages in the hands of irresponsible people, I have frequently heard such remarks as the following from the attendants: "Who is the best judge of the propriety of restraining a patient, the physician who only sees the person for a few moments each day, when of course the patient knows enough to be quiet, or 'us attendants?'" "Knows enough to be quiet!" — knows enough always to feel that in a kind and considerate physician they have a "friend at court," and it is well indeed not to give this authority into the hands of persons who do *not* know enough to be trusted; to remember that these persons, so unfortunate as to be obliged to stay there, are human. I well remember the last person "camisoled" on our ward. Her "delusion" was, that she was the wife of her physician at home, and, as was frequently the case, she was very indignant that the people around her would not call her by his name instead of her own married name. One of the rules of the asylum was, "use every effort to quiet, and above all, do not taunt any patient in reference to their "delusions," however unreasonable." One evening, just before supper, one of the attendants — "our musician" — was sitting at the piano, and this woman was standing at one side near her, listening, when she looked up and made a vile, insulting remark, regarding her '"delusion," in connection with this physician. I was sitting so as to be able to see them both, and I never saw such, an intense look of anger as on that woman's face as she sprang at the attendant's throat, and hissed, "I'll have your life for that!" And her life she would have had (and small pity), only that her partner, and several of the patients ran to her assistance. Immediately, word was telephoned to the office for permission and help to "camisole" Mrs. K. Poor soul! she died not long after, and I never saw any one make as brave a struggle as she, against that "restraint," and it was only accomplished through the combined strength of four. After she was conquered, and rendered still more helpless, by being locked in her room, this cowardly fiend, in the person of her attendant, stood outside the door and drove her into positive frenzy by her sneering taunts at her fruitless attempt on her life, and the following morning she was transferred to a back ward, because Madame C. was afraid of her. Shortly after this, upon coming out of the dining-room, I turned to the sink for the purpose of getting a drink of water, when she snatched the glass out of my hand, and pushed me out in the hall, upon which I turned upon her, and said, "Water should be free, even though you do stint the patients in the use of tea and soap, to supply your mother at home." She had a habit of losing color when surprised, and she was white as she turned to her partner and said, "Good heavens! did you hear that?" And after a little she said, "Come on now, I'm going out there and just scare the life out of her." And out they came, and they jerked my chair around, and seized my hands as usual, but before they could give them a "twist," I let them know there were other disclosures I could make — explanations of the mysterious disappearances of more important and valuable "State articles" than tea and soap — and they left me, considering "discretion, in that case, the better part of valor." And after that, when in the vicinity of the "devil's corner," they whispered. I do not entirely disapprove of the use of certain constraints; indeed, at times, under judicious persons, I consider them a kindness. I know there were nights when it would have been a merciful act to lock me in a "crib," so that I could not have gotten out. The "cribs" were simply a bedstead (such as we all used), with a lid over it. But there were a number of those same old "cribs," that added bloody brilliancy to that historical bonfire. As in old houses, there cluster many memories — so with these "old cribs." They had been moving objects for many years, and had the way only have been smoothed for them, I'm thinking they might have walked, unassisted, out to that funeral pyre — though whether or no they would have cast themselves into the fire, "deponent sayeth not."

CHAPTER XIII.

At last I reached that blessed mood,
In which the burden of the mystery,
In which the heavy, weary weight,
Of all this unintelligible woe
Was lightened. — Wadsworth.

As I proceed with these reminiscences, some of them so fraught with painful, mortifying memories, I recognize more and more the difficulty and delicacy of the task undertaken, lest I may be charged with entertaining a feeling of malice toward my attendant. And while most earnestly protesting against the charge, I freely admit I have not the slightest charity for one of the class, by comparison, with the universal sympathy I feel for those under their charge. There are good, conscientious girls occupying this position, but "'tis pitiful, 'tis wondrous pitiful" that they are so rare. Strange, too, that they do not sometimes stop and think, "possibly I may sometime come here a patient." Once I heard two of my attendants talking of the responsibility of their position, and one of them said, "Well, sometimes I feel as though I was almost insane myself. I take no pleasure in 'my days off.' Even when I go to the city I am thinking all the time of my ward; am afraid some thing may go wrong in my absence." And the other one replied, "Well, you are a fool, I stay here for sixteen dollars a month exactly, and when I hang up my key in the office on my way to the city, I leave the hospital and these 'nasty things' behind." The "nasty things" were the patients under her care. Such "exclusives" should seek more congenial surroundings, and would, I presume, only that they could no place else so easily earn (?) sixteen or eighteen dollars per month.

The events narrated in several preceding chapters, bring me to another change of administration, the contemplation of which caused me but little thought. During almost all of the past four years I had been so utterly miserable as not to be willing to respond to Dr. Rogers' repeated attempts at kindness, and had formed no attachments for any one particularly. Death had removed my enemy, and he was succeeded by Dr. Thomas, a gentleman who soon made his presence and influence felt, and who was the one remaining member of the outgoing administration. Through his kindness my surroundings had already been made more comfortable, and though keenly appreciating his attentions, I had not yet been able in the slightest to respond to them. My particular dread of the incoming administration was that I must again submit to be called upon to run the gauntlet of criticism for another four years by the new superintendent and his friends; for I was still an object of curious study and speculation, and not at all an agreeable sort of individual either in appearance or manner, and had not yet been able to respond in the slightest manner to the polite notice and respectful, silent acts of kindness, from the presiding physician, Dr. Thomas. It was known to all of us that the new superintendent and his family were in the building, and all were expecting him daily to make his entry with the dignity of former proceedings of the sort, but several days passed and he came not. On Sunday morning of June seventh, 1883, while the attendants were preparing the patients for their usual walk, and I, together with several other old clods, was waiting to be taken across the hall into another ward to stay until their return, the back door very near "my corner" opened, and a gentleman came in alone, walking up to me, he said, pleasantly, at the same time extending his hand, "How do you do this morning?" I had not the most remote idea whom he was, neither would it have made the slightest difference if I had known. He had offered me his hand, and, of course, was simply mocking my well-known "delusion." Every body, I thought, knew that my hand was accursed, so roughly turning away, I said, "Oh you go to hell," my favorite place of consignment. He looked at me just for an instant as though utterly confounded, and said, "Go where?" in a perfectly exasperating tone; then pausing a moment, said, "No, indeed, I won't go there; I don't believe I should like that climate. And now, then," he continued, "wouldn't you like to go out riding or walking this lovely morning?" and I said "No." Then he said, "What's the matter with you any way? Do you know what you do want?" And I, growing more angry every moment, said, "There's nothing at all the matter with me, and I want you to go about your business, and let me alone." Then his manner changed, and he said, decidedly, "That's exactly what I don't intend to do. It is my business not to let you alone any longer. I understand you have not had your foot upon the ground in two years. Why, that's dreadful. Now then, inside of ten minutes, I will bring my porter, and he and O will pick you up, rocking chair and all, and carry you down stairs," and off he went. And this was my introduction to Dr. Fletcher, our new superintendent. Did he execute his threat? A moment or so after, our supervisoress, a young lady whom I had always liked, came bringing a hat, which she began trying on me, saying kindly, "Are you going to allow Dr. Fletcher to make such a spectacle of you as that?" And I answered, "Does he think I am a damned fool?" "No," she answered, "he thinks you a very determined, obstinate woman, and you will find him equally as determined. Now, do come with me," and giving me her arm, we walked down stairs. This was the man under whose humane management I remained until well. The proof of which was a discharge to myself, at my own solicitation, "as a person of sound mind, competent to control my own actions and affairs," instead of being discharged to my county, subject to the sheriff's action; in which case I would become either the "poor house" pauper, which my husband intended, or be a dependent upon the charity of my relations. I am neither; thanks to the humanity of honorable men who aided me in my determination to demand my rights unforfeited through any fault save that of misfortune. And I am again a free woman—and strong in my sense of outraged motherhood, am looking forward hopefully to the time when free from present surroundings, my children will claim their mother again. Do not understand that I was immediately restored. My convalescence was slow, and attended by many painful, mortifying scenes, the memory of which even now brings the blush of wounded feeling to my cheek. I was so often, so horribly misunderstood. Probably the perusal of extracts from letters written to my sister and others during my early convalescence, all of which were preserved and returned to me after my complete recovery, will better explain my peculiar state of mind than any thing I now say. All women know the luxury of tears, as well as men misunderstand them. But for five years not a tear came to relieve my sorrow or moisten my burning eyes. And to my dying hour I will remember when they came thick and fast with choking sobs — and what a blessed relief they were too. All from a kind voice saying, "Mrs. Agnew, is there any thing I can do to make your sad surroundings pleasanter; and will you promise not to hesitate to ask me for any favor within my power to grant?" I could not answer for tears. Call this childish weakness, if you please. I was more helpless than a child, in my loss of self-control, and I had so long been unused to kindness. Dr. Thomas, the kind, considerate friend referred to, deserves the confidence of all having the welfare of the afflicted at heart, and he has the affectionate regard of all his patients. One morning, as he was making his usual "morning rounds," he asked my attendant to bring him a chair, saying as he seated himself by my rocking-chair, "You need not wait here, I want to have a talk with Mrs. Agnew." Good heavens, a talk with me! I was terribly frightened. No one ever talked with me; they only talked at and about me, and I knew not what to expect, but his manner was kind, and he began, "I want to talk to you this morning about that terrible 'night medicine' to which you have become such a slave" (a preparation of chloral given to produce sleep). "Why," he said, "when I examined the report of the 'night watch' this morning, I was absolutely shocked at the amount of that miserable stuff given you last night. Do you know that the last dose given you would have killed me, strong man as I am; and I presume it had only the effect of confusing you, making you drunk. Now then, listen to me. That medicine won't kill you, but its continued use will make you a miserable imbecile, and you don't want to become that; you want to get well and go home to your family. Now there's no doubt about your will power to stop this right straight off, and I want your promise this morning that you will never again ask the 'night watch' for another single drop. Once you make this promise, and I believe you are just the woman to keep your word, and in return I pledge you my word that I will instruct the 'night watch' to give you all you wish if you do ask for it." And he said farther, "I must tell you that you are undertaking a great struggle. It will be far worse than the drunkard stopping drink. You may be reduced to the weakness of an infant, but we will all help yon, give you our sympathy, and sometime you will thank me for my effort to save you." I promised him I would try, and I succeeded. I doubt that prayers of mine would avail to shower down blessings upon his head, but certainly if in the present or future my restored intellect and sound body adds happiness to any friend of mine, they will join me in my sincere affection and gratitude to him. In my extremity I had a friend. I will not attempt a description of my agony of mind and body before the victory was complete; the recollections are too painful. Those who have fought and conquered the "opium habit" may have some conception of the state of complete prostration to which I was reduced. And my sufferings have made me more tolerant in my condemnation of any weakness of poor humanity. Afterward I asked permission of the doctor to read Luther Benson's "Fifteen Years in Hell," feeling that I could fully sympathize with the author in his attempt at describing his feelings when fighting the demons of delirium tremens.

I had become almost blind from its continued use, and could not, therefore, gratify my returning love for reading, when again my friend came to my rescue. Was he a mind reader? He asked me one day if he should not send me something from his library, and I told him I could not see to read. Then he said, "Won't you go with me to my office and select a pair of glasses?" And I, startled at the very thought of going out among people, said, "Oh, no." Then he said, "Well, will you wear a pair of them if I send them to you?" And I said, "Yes." Only a few months before, when our new superintendent came into office, his wife, occupying the position of matron, came into our ward with some company, and coming up to "my corner," said, "This lady always sets right here, and does not wish to be spoken to, or noticed in any way." A gentleman in the company, an old physician, said, as he attempted to place his hand upon my head, "So she finds her own thoughts sufficient company, does she; and scorns all other?" I could not reply, but had he put his hand upon me, I certainly should have struck him, but I turned to her and said, desperately, "Oh, I wish you would let me alone." And she said, in her quiet, kind manner as she turned away, "Well, I will let you alone, poor woman." Now see the wise policy of the doctor. He knew how rudely I had repulsed Mrs. Fletcher, and the same evening asked her to bring me the glasses as a test, I presume, of my improved politeness. I had gotten over considerable of my "meanness" by that time, and received them from her as kindly as they were presented, thanking her most heartily. Dear, noble, self-sacrificing woman; I learned, ere long, to love her. We had much in common in the way of congenial thought together with favorite authors, and no book in her elegant selection escaped my penciling, not objected to by their owner, since as she said, "Your marks add interest to my books, as I can better judge of your peculiar liking for certain sentiments." And I became a perfect devourer of literary matter, after my mental starvation of so many years. And when at a later period of my convalescence, I went to her in heart-breaking sorrow, she took me into her arms and tried to comfort me, as only a great hearted, unselfish woman can do. And in the struggle that followed, when for a time it seemed that the waves of mental darkness might again overwhelm me before I had regained sufficient bodily health to attempt the contest of my right to see my children, she stood by me a very pillar of strength — and I conquered. It matters not what the future hold for me, nothing can take from me the sweet memory of that meeting, when my three little boys rushed into my arms, with tears and smiles, struggling for the ascendency, repeating over and again, as though glad of the opportunity to use the dear name of mother, "Mamma, mamma, don't cry so, we are so glad to see you." Glad to see me; and was I not glad too, after seven years of cruel separation! Spite of bitter persecution — against all influence brought to bear upon those children to induce them to believe either they had no mother, or that she had willfully, wickedly forsaken them; had gotten tired of her home, of her family had lost, or had never possessed the instincts of wife or mother; "had deliberately planned this whole matter;" had willingly gone to the asylum, where for seven years she had "feigned insanity" — spite of all this, when "mamma," strong in her love for her children, through her own determination, was granted permission to test her children's memory, she had her blessed reward. By persistent searching, repeated tests, she received assurance that through all, her children remembered their mother, as she was, before this trouble came, and too, that they would gladly have her back to stay with them always. But it was not to be. It might *not* have been, or it *would* be.

CHAPTER XIV.

Oft in the stilly night, e'er slumber's
Chain has bound me,
Fond memory brings the light
Of other days around me. — Tom Moore.

After writing to my sister the letter of renunciation spoken of
in a preceding chapter, I neither received nor wrote a letter
until November of 1883. My sister having been in constant
correspondence with Dr. Thomas, wrote to me by his advice,
saying so many letters had been sent me without a word of
reply, but that she felt now that surely I would send her a line,
and that then she would write at length, of many changes,
some of them very sad, that had transpired during my years
of silence. Her letter touched me deeply. This, my youngest
sister, and my favorite, was together with her husband, the
only exceptions among my relatives who did not see me
during the three years of my "peculiarities" before I was
confined in the asylum, and I felt more kindly toward them,
than any others of my family. And too, they had both visited
me since my incarceration, coming from their home in
Pittsburg, Penn. But I had gotten so completely unaccustomed
to writing, that I felt but little inclination to reply to her letter,
until in answer to the doctor's question, "are you going to
write to your sister?" I said, No! And he answered "Now! I am
disappointed in you! If you could read the number of good
letters I have read from that good sister about you, certainly
you would send her, if no more, a line to relieve her of long
waiting, and I have assured her you would write." And so I
wrote November 26, 1883: "I don't know if I am better or not;
certainly there's a little pressure lifted some where, for I can
cry now! Not as I used to, for days together, 'making myself
and every body in the house miserable.' Tell mother, if she is
still living, that it was ignorance of myself and not willful

wickedness that made 'Dottie' give her more trouble than all the rest of her children." This was all, just this short note, whose reception caused both pain and pleasure. And a speedy reply came telling me of sad changes indeed! Death had been doing his usual work among my friends — had come into our own home circle, and had taken a sister and a dearly loved aunt, and then truly I sadly realized my "death in life," and I answered in regard to a sentence in my former note, that wounded my mother's feelings. I had no intention of hurting mother. I have never doubted but that she loved her children! even her "black sheep;" but if I write at all, I must not be restricted, I will write just as I feel. Do I not remember "sharp, impatient words spoken to my children, and deeply regretted?" No! I do not! We are not apt to speak sharp impatient words to our babies! We are more apt to love them for their helplessness, and my children were but babies when I was separated from them; I had nut time to become impatient with them. And of my sister's death, I wrote, "Poor Mary! I have dreamed so often of her and of Eugene; I never think of them separately, and if I could but fix the date, I believe I had a dream that was a premonition of her death. It was about the middle of September, the month she died, I thought I was standing watching them transplanting a large plant of Cape Jessamine, covered with its lovely creamy bloom; and as she stooped to lift it, said, 'Oh, this horrible pain!' and sunk down at my feet. I awakened with her voice yet sounding in my ears, and I believe just at that moment she was dying. Oh! I hope some kind hand put white flowers in her coffin, and upon it, for few ever went to their grave in Moscow without flowers, which she so loved and carefully tended from her generous hand. And how her life was saddened by the one shadow amidst the fitful sunshine around her own hearthstone. She believed in prayer. I can see her now and hear her voice, as she supplicated, almost in agony, when she little thought any eye was upon her, save his alone to whom she prayed, first for her own loved ones, and that the shadow might be removed from me, her afflicted sister. Yet in life her prayers were not answered. She too, must wait until 'after a while,' for compensation for years of sorrow. Does she now know why?" After I had once overcome my feeling against writing, I took a sort of comfort in thus giving expression to my feelings. My writing did not always consist of letters, and I regret now that some of my scraps were not preserved; they would be valuable as specimens of "crazy literature." I will transcribe one written to my physician in defense of my attendants whom the doctor was inclined to blame, since the facts of the case had been misrepresented to him, and I am always glad of the opportunity of speaking favorably of faithful attendants. My only apology for its erratic nature is its date, Friday morning, Dec. 7, 1883:

"I have another writing spell on me this morning. The spell has been on since yesterday morning, when we had the fight on the 'fourth ward.' I never saw human beings fight as they did! I saw once in my life, two dogs fighting. They fought up street and down street, out to the bank and over it, down to the water edge, and one of the dogs was dead when the fight was over. I was in my room and heard an uproar in the hall and went out just as Hattie C. came screaming around the corner of the short hall, flying to the dining-room for protection, which she had only just entered and slammed the door, when Mary H. came snorting around the corner, making a rush for the water pitcher standing on the table, which Miss K. snatched, and held on to, howling, 'Let me get at her! God damn her! I will kill her! I will kill her!' Just then Miss H. opened the dining-room door to come to Miss K.'s assistance, and Hattie looked out, and then Mary H. gripped one hand in her hair and planted her other fist squarely in that poor girl's forehead; and she fell, Mary on top, and there she fought with one fist, and Hattie panting and strangling, begging, 'Oh! girls for God's sake! don't let her kill me!' And the girls, both of them, white as death, doing all in their power to loosen her hold. Presently, Sarah N. came to help; some one, and 'Aunt Betty' came to me and said, 'Oh, Mrs. Agnew, that poor Hattie will be killed!' and I ran down the hall for Miss C., who is strong, and though she thinks she owns this place, and once in a while strikes any and every body will always help the attendants when they need it, and I tell you they needed help, then! Well, Mrs. W. came soon to the fore, and was promptly ordered (and rightly, too) to 'go about her business,' and after awhile they were separated some way, and while both the girls were holding Mary, Sarah seized a chair, and if one of them had not let go of Mary for a moment and seized Sarah, I'm thinking Mary H. would very likely, then and there, have 'crossed the river.' After the chair was taken from her, or at the time, Alice L. got excited and pitched into Miss H., and then I went to Sarah and put my arms around her to hold her while 'the girls' put Mary in her room, and locked the door. Sarah didn't fight, or attempt to fight me, but she broke away from me, and sent that chair spinning down the hall, and she after it, when she broke it into splinters, and so the fight ended, but the effects of it lasted all day; and with me all night. I don't know how the fight began, but I have a pretty good idea of its beginning. I go to the wash room now in my night clothing, for I am afraid of Mary H.'s bodily strength, and I guess you would be too, if you could once see her 'kick the waddin'' out of some body, as I have seen her try to do by every body on this ward that she dared to. When I was moved from the front table for 'sassing' nice old Aunty W., I told Miss K. I didn't care a damn if she did make me leave the front table. I was seated beside Mary H., and I have always eaten that 'stew' we have for breakfast, and sometimes cold winter mornings it tastes real nice. But I got tired of seeing her, after drinking half dozen, more or less, cups of coffee, use the dish of 'stew' for a slop bowl, and I said, 'If you empty your coffee grounds into that meat dish to-morrow morning, Mary H., just as sure as you live, I'll slap your mouth!' Good Lord! you should have heard her! 'Don't you dare call me Mary, you call me Miss H., and I *will* empty my coffee grounds there! nobody but a fool or a hog would eat that stuff!' And I said, 'Well, just you try it to-morrow morning if you dare!' And she said. 'I will too! and I'll knock you down and kick the 'stuffin'out of you too, I will,' and I wouldn't have cared then if she had killed me — I think I would have been rather thankful than otherwise; and besides, my h'English wasn't going to stand any h'Irish h'impudence. But the next morning every thing was lovely at the back table, and since then Mary has quite occasionally, so to speak, eaten the 'stew' herself, juicy, tender beefsteak, such as she has always been accustomed to in her capacity (formerly) of servant girl, not being at all times forthcoming. One morning, Mattie La. was 'carrying on' at the first table, and Mary said, under her breath, 'I'll just kick that thing to death this morning!' and just outside of the dining-room door, she *downed* her, and when 'the girls' reached her, and carried her and laid her on a lounge, she could only just groan; and when they asked, 'who did this?' Mrs. 'Rutherford B. Hayes,' whom she has knocked down and kicked more than once (and did you ever see her foot?) answered, 'It was Mary H., that devil, did it!' and 'Mrs. Hayes' trembling so she could scarcely stand, had been trying to lift Mattie up before 'the girls' reached her. Only a few weeks since, I was standing at one basin in the wash-room, and some one else at the other one, and a good many others waiting their turn, when in walked Mary H. with 'Oh, for God's sake! every Irish and Dutch thing in the house crowded in here, when I want to wash!' I was through, and I said, 'Well, I know one Irishman who had better walk back then, to her room until the ladies are all done,' and she came up to me with her fist doubled and said, 'I told you never to speak to me, didn't I?' and I said, 'I didn't mind you, did I?' and she stood there shaking her fist right in my face, and pawing the floor (she wanted to kick awfully) and I looked her straight in the eye, and said, 'Don't you dare strike me, Mary,' and she turned and bounced into her room, and banged the door. I was so weak and nervous before I reached mine, that I walked like a drunken person. Another time at dinner, Alice L. had the sugar-bowl in her hand fooling with it, putting it down and picking it up, touching it. I wanted some sugar and asked her several times for it, and then took it out of her hand (she was setting at the foot of the table), that made her mad and she threw the lid of the bowl at me, breaking my cup and spilling the contents over the table, making considerable racket. Mary H. had her nose in her plate eating, and did not see a thing of it, but when Miss K. came back and said, 'See here, what is all this fuss about?' Mary said, 'Its this thing, jist; she's all the time making such a fuss, as none of us ladies can eat at all.' And I said, 'You're a liar!' I don't know if I said a God damned liar, or not, very likely I did, for I wasn't very choice in my language when up to the boiling point; I never was. And she said, 'Me lie! an angel in heaven would sooner lie; and you shut your mouth, or Miss K. and me will both take you down and just 'cuisi' the waddin' out of ye,' (I'd like to know if that word 'cuisi' is pure unadulterated Irish? It certainly isn't English, possibly though it's Latin or Greek). And Miss K. said, quietly, 'Let her alone, Mary, don't talk to her.' Another time, Alice McC. laid her lengthened sweetness from her end of the table to mine, and quick as a flash, snatched the 'milk can' out of my hand, and pouring the milk into her cup, threw the empty can back at me, which I, in return, aimed straight at her old shaved pate, but missing that, upset her cup, spilling the contents all over Auntie H., (our telephone), and I was real sorry it went on her. Then there was the usual uproar, and all agreed that, beyond a doubt, 'the devil sat at meat' at the back table. One day I did really and truly break a pepper box accidentally; I can swear to that fact if necessary, and I was awfully tempted to take that pepper box up to the attendants' table and confess I broke it, and when Miss K. came to gather up the knives and forks, and I, as usual, *threw* mine at her, she looked at the broken box, but said nothing, and wonderful to relate, nobody told her I broke it.

Mary, as a general thing, forgets it is Friday until after she has eaten all the meat she can get that suits her, then she remembers, and says she will tell the Lord she is sorry, and he will forgive her. Intelligent Catholics eat meat on Friday if they choose, and Mary knows this. She is far from being an ignorant girl, only she wishes to appear saintly; and her constant threat is, 'I'll tell the doctor and he will believe me because he is a Catholic.' Dr. Thomas, I know you are a Catholic — have known it ever since the change of administration in 1879, but if on that account you are influenced in your treatment of the unfortunates under your charge, I am mistaken in my estimate of your character; I don't believe it; I don't know any thing of the Catholic religion; I never was inside of one of your churches but twice, once in the cathedral, at Philadelphia, where I listened with wonder to the chanting of mass by the priest at the altar, and the responses of the choir, charmed with the beautiful music, and after service being shown all through the vast building with its splendid paintings. I really know nothing of your religion; do not know if the reference to 'probation after death' in the sermon on 'Mischief of a Fractional Orthodoxy' means Catholicism or not, but would like to know if it does or not. The fact of the business is, I don't know any thing of any religion. I only know if there's a hell, there's where I am going sometime. I like this sermon for its independence, and it is certainly original. I don't think that 'Rev. Joseph Cook' will in any probability find any one daring enough to order him what he shall believe, and believing say. We used to live opposite the Catholic church in Seymour, and I knew 'Father Schenck,' the young German priest, and one of the sisters. They took our house when we left it, and when 'Kye' was sick, and I nursed him in a darkened room for three weeks, 'Fadder Yank,' as he called him, called frequently at the door to ask after the 'little sick boy,' and as soon as he was able, came with his buggy and took him out driving. Do you think I have not a warm spot in my heart for him? And 'Sister Mary Stanislaus' was the first familiar face I saw after coming to the asylum. I called her as she was passing through the ward, and she came to me with extended hand, saying, 'I am so surprised; where are your husband and children?' But I couldn't take her hand, and I was crying so, I could not speak, and there were tears in her eyes if they did not fall. I planted a vine at that house, and trained it over the porch, and have some very sweet memories, and some very sad ones, too, of my life there. 'Willie,' my baby was born there. I know nothing of your religion, and yet it was strangely mixed up in my ravings; and I remember thinking Mrs. C. was my sister. I know Mrs. C. is your sister-in-law, and I know too that I am possibly laying myself liable to misconstruction in thus writing, but I don't care; I am writing honestly, and shall sign my name when I am through. Mrs. C. used to come slipping into my room so often, and would be standing by my side before I knew she was there, and several times she called me 'mother.' One evening she came and stood by my side for a little while, and laying her hand upon my shoulder, said, 'I do so believe you are my mother,' and tried to kiss me. I would not allow her to kiss me, but I took her in my arms and rocked her to sleep. And I hid her 'wristlets' when we were all out walking, and she was strapped to a tree. I told her attendant I had hidden them, and she tried to induce me to tell where, saying it was necessary she should be 'restrained;' that her husband knew of it, etc., and I told her that might all be true, but I would not tell where they were. And I don't know if they ever were found. I never went near the spot again, for I knew I was being watched. I had a piece of her shawl that she gave me around me when my husband came to see me in Dec, 1879, and when he was leaving he shook hands with Miss L, twice, since she was so very profuse in her offers to do any thing in her power for 'him or his,' and she kept and ate all the oranges he brought me. That was just before I went out of my senses the first time, and after that 'came the deluge,' or some thing. I never read any thing so fine as that 'Widow's Mite,' and I read

'In the dusk,' too, and I tell you, Dr. Thomas, you are probing deeper than any mortal knows. I'm getting a glimmer of what the 'secret known only to the Jews' means. You are not a Mason; Catholics are never so. Masonry was instituted at the building of Solomon's temple. The Jews built that, didn't they? But I started out to tell you about the fight. Don't understand that I hate Mary. I don't at all. She says she is going home Christmas, if the Lord don't take her sooner. Well, I hope she may go, but if the Lord wants her, I hope he will know better how to manage her than 'the girls' on the fourth ward did, and when she wants to kick somebody out of heaven, she will be restrained by a kind and merciful God, who made her as crazy as ever 'Dr. Walker's bed-bug' was. Dr. Walker was a Mason, wasn't he? She won't even threaten to kick me out; I won't be there ever, I'll be in the other place, wherever or whatever that be. Not in literal fire and brimstone; I don't believe any such stuff as that, but I'll be in hell. There are degrees, several sorts, including the degrees of insanity.

Respectfully,

Mrs. Agnew."

CHAPTER XV.

The above letter was preserved and returned to me for publication, and is a very good example of my state of mind when written. Generally, my scraps were thrown out of my window, and become the prey of the "garbage gang," who, with their brooms and the "police wheelbarrow," made daily rounds outside. I will give an extract from a letter to my sister about the same date as the above: "God Almighty; how I hate that man," referring to the physician so frequently mentioned in these pages. I hated him while living, and I hate him dead. I watched that man die. Oh no, I did not regularly observe his pulse, but I heard his labored breathing, and watched his step grow heavy and languid with weakness, until one day I heard he was dead. My enemy was gone, and though I gave no sign of joy, no one but myself was aware why I made such a guy of my already 'awful looking' self, as to cut my hair in straggling strings and clips, and scollops, so that it had almost to be shaved in consequence. This was the outward expression of my inward joy! My flag of victory! Since he had continuously refused my repeated requests to have my hair cut to relieve my aching head. He and his 'right bowers' are both gone. Once she met him as he was entering the door near me, and as he made this remark, pointing to me with a backward turn of the thumb, 'There's a fine subject for the dissecting table,' answered with a 'Ha! ha! she is so!' It matters little what becomes of my miserable body. It may find its way to the dissecting table, but he, thank God! won't have a hand in it. And I hope most earnestly these two worthies are not divided in death. Some enterprising disciple of Aesculapius should secure their anatomy, have them nicely articulated — dental arrangements — complete hers with gold fillings to simulate nature. They should occupy the same office, grinning at each other 'through all eternity' 'Male and female, created he, them.'" This letter was written during the first year of convalescence, and I offer no other apology for its bitterness. In another, after being requested to say something regarding my daily life, I wrote: "This place reminds me of a great clock, so perfectly regular and smooth are its workings, and certainly any latent bump of order stands a good chance of development here. The system is perfect: our bill of fare is excellent, and varied, as in any well regulated family, and especially, we have good bread. We retire at the ringing of the telephone at eight o'clock, and an hour later, there's darkness and silence that can almost be felt all over this vast building, excepting an occasional piercing cry from some restless soul not yet under the kindly influence of 'night medicine.' And the silence is scarcely disturbed by the light, careful step of the 'night watch,' as she makes her half hour rounds. Flitting quickly along, she throws the penetrating light of her tiny lantern into each room through the 'elliptical openings' in the panels, ready at the slightest sound from the inmates to respond with kindly inquiry of 'What's wanting there?' And as I lay there, hour after hour, thinking—for I am yet a poor sleeper—my mind goes longingly back to the past; way back to my childhood, stopping here and there to cull a flower from some sweet memory; dropping a tear over the grave of some cherished hope unfulfilled; smiling over the memory of some childish grief, then, seemingly, so hard to bear, now so trivial, by comparison with present trouble, alas, so real! I am with my dear ones again; feel my precious children's innocent kisses upon my lips, hear again my husband's voice, always kind and gentle to me before this trouble, until after a time I became nervous, and begin to talk and listen to the ward clock talking, and the wonderful things this old clock tells me! The remarkable confidences we do exchange; don't expect me to tell you the half of them. As I say, you will keep my secrets good, old clock; you will never tell! tell! tell! The refrain of never! never! forever! ever! ever continues, until through sheer impatience of my inability to stop that clock's tongue, after I am tired of talking, I spring out of bed and pace the floor, trying not to listen to its never ending gossiping clatter. Even a clock as a companion sometimes grows tiresome. After awhile though, the ting-a-ling-ling of the ward telephone says, 'Get up, it is five o'clock in the morning,' and the same old routine begins again; and I'd like you to find a busier or as funny a scene, as an early morning on an insane ward — women in all stages of deshabille are running here and there, fussing and spatting over disputed articles of wearing apparel, in some cases monopolizing their own and their neighbors' outfit. Plenty of time is given us to make our not elaborate toilet. Plenty of soap and water, hot and cold. An abundance of clean towels, combs and brushes; and when the breakfast bell summons us to the dining-room, no one need complain of the breakfast that greets us — though in the winter sometimes we do get fearfully tired of the perfect regularity with which a certain 'meat stew' makes its appearance. Almost any luxury (?) becomes sort of monotonous after six or seven years' indulgence, and we earnestly hoped last winter when the kitchen burned, that its valuable recipe was consumed, but was informed by our careful druggist that he could furnish a duplicate, since all valuable concoctions, such as that 'stew,' are religiously preserved." This last paragraph was an after-thought, not included in my letter to my sister. After breakfast every "lady" who is able and willing for duty goes to work, every body knowing exactly what to do, and none daring to infringe upon her neighbors' territory, or fancied right, for I assure you they are quite as tenacious of their rights, and far more so of their dignity than many of their sane sisters "outside the bars" — after a while the ward is completely put to rights, and in splendid order, too, without the slightest disagreement or disorder, with only an occasional "come, come, 'ladies,' not quite so noisy!" from the attendant. But quite frequently some "servant" will give an impertinant reply to some important "mistress of this house, I'll have you understand!" — said mistress, as is frequently the case in the best regulated families, having gotten up "out of sorts," or as

we in asylum parlance say, "a little off," — when presto,
change! and scrubbing buckets, mops, broom-sticks and what
not! any thing that serves for a weapon, comes into active use,
to say nothing of tongues! But unlike our sane sisters outside,
we can't order our sassy servants to "pack up their traps and
leave, and we will do our work ourselves." No indeed!
"servants" and "mistresses" are on a complete level here, but
generally, on our ward we are a quite orderly crowd now,
since "the devil's corner" is vacated, and to its former
occupant has come glimmerings of the "promised
millennium," and she is daily learning new lessons of faith in
humanity independent of creeds, or established religion.

CHAPTER XVI.

"Oh, that mine enemy might write a book!"

A LETTER sometimes serves equally as well to bless or damn its author. My readers will please bear in mind that I quote these extracts from letters to give a true idea of the condition of my mind before having gotten sufficient control of myself as to be politic—a trait of character conservative and safe, and one that numerous friends of mine, careful of my interests, advise me to cultivate, since this seems not to have been one of my original endowments. It may be a misfortune to have too much of the positive in one's composition, but in transcribing these unstudied utterances of an unsettled mind I feel very little inclination to differ materially from the sentiments they contain. My own individuality, the one thing I must maintain, glimmers through them all, even the craziest of them!

In a letter from my sister, in which she asks: "What do you mean by night medicine?" "Have you ever been a victim of opiates?" I did not know until a year later that my husband, in a letter to my sister, charged me with being also an "opium eater," a drug I never even so much as tasted, to my knowledge, and I answered her thus: "Night medicine" is a preparation of chloral, and it was given me the first night I spent in this place, and has been continued every night since, excepting as occasionally it would occur to Dr. Walker that probably I might be deriving some comfort from its use, and he would discontinue its use for a time. At such periods I was wild and wretched in the extreme! Not that it served its purpose with me—that of producing sleep! It simply kept mo from continuous thought, and kept me in bed too, since its effect upon me was to make me drunk—so that I would fall helpless upon the floor, unable, without the assistance of the "night watch," to get up again. But deprived of it, all night long I would walk the floor wringing my hands, with my familiar spirit ever by my side, with its horrible accusations repeated, and met by denial on my part until worn out, and desperate, I would make confession of sins, only slightly conceived of, in my real mind. Then would follow the taunting voice: "Why don't you kill your worthless self, then? Why don't you? Others have done this, why not you? You don't dare to! You shall not! You shall live, and live! You shall never die!" And all this time just outside my door, whereon moonlight nights I could plainly see it, standing upon the table was the "night medicine," which if I could only, Oh God! if I only could get it once, alone! I could drink myself to death and forgetfulness of all this misery. But at such times not one drop could I beg, even to scatter these desperate thoughts. All I could do was to stand at the door, with my face pressed through the openings, gazing at my hope of nepenthe and cursing that villainous doctor!

Before mechanical restraints had been entirely dispensed with, the large wooden chair, used for the purpose of subduing unruly patients, was in my room. This chair was secured to the floor, and at the back was an opening, through which, after being passed around the patient's waist, a leather strap was passed through and fastened. I had never been restrained in this chair, but during these sleepless nights that chair actually haunted me! It was never vacant! One or another of my former friends or enemies came and sat there without speaking, and I would go cautiously up to them and put out my hand to touch them, and they were gone! Again, my familiar spirit (I called this spirit my conscience) would be seated there, calling upon me to give account of every word and deed. Or I was ordered to get out of bed and sit there myself, at the judgment seat! And times without number I was commanded to tear a strip off my bed clothing and tie myself in the chair. And I never thought of disobeying that voice! I was considerably more obedient to that inner voice than to "our young ladies," who kept house for us on the ward.

In another letter of later date, I wrote: "You have no idea of the celebrities we have here in our boarding-house." First and eldest is "Aunt Betty" B, who is everybody's "Aunt Betty" when at her normally insane self, but who at her times of excitement—which are quite frequent, is "Mrs. Elizabeth B! I thank you! Don't you dare Aunt Betty me I And I'm no pauper I'll have you to understand! I could buy you and all your kit if you were black! And its none of your infernal business if I have been here twenty years! You don't pay my bills!" On her annual or semi-annual "tears," in hospital slang, she demolishes every thing perishable in her "old curiosity shop," as her room with its miscellaneous collection of odds and ends, may well be called, and as she goes tearing up and down the hall, with her thin, straggling gray hair, which she is everlastingly trying to comb, flying in all directions, her clothing hanging in tatters upon her, and her feet thrust into the doctor's old slippers. Often she looks but little like the tidy, ruffled-aproned, good tempered "Aunt Betty" that everybody knows and is kind to, and "Mrs. President Hayes" has boarded here for ten years, and all this time her husband reigns at Washington, and she can't imagine why he does not allow her to go there too, and take her rightful position as "first lady of the land." Of course she can't see why, poor woman! and I am afraid she never will understand why this is thus, tho' by birth and education she is not unfitted to fill such a position. And her rival, whom the latter holds in supreme contempt on account of her "delusion," is "Mrs. ex-President Arthur," who confidently expects "Chester" to come for her as soon as he also vacates the Presidential chair, and she looks forward to the time when it will be her supreme bliss to bestow upon him her untold millions, since she fears he may not have an abundance left after the extravagances of his term at the White House. And "Gov. Wood," I really forget whom she succeeded. But she is not the least important personage on the ward. If you could see her at the piano! Every nerve in my body gets upon edge and enters quivering protest against the horrid discord as she daily practices (?) twoblessed hours! Not a note, or a chord does she know! But there she sits like a great owl peering through her glasses, music book before her, apeing the most elaborate manner of playing, making difficult (?) runs, crossing her hands and invariably playing through the book at one sitting. But she is quite valuable help to the "young ladies,"and they allow her all sorts of privileges at the expense of tortured nerves. About the handsomest old lady and important — who wouldn't be important holding such a position — (?) I ever saw, is the "Autocrat" of our dining-room. Auntie H. She is employed at an annual salary of eighty millions to superintend the workings of the universe, as pertains to earthly affairs, but does not aspire to heavenly matters. Her headquarters are here, and her agents, tried and true, are scattered through the "uttermost parts of the earth," and she receives and responds to their constant reports by telephone. As a consequence of such extended territory, and the importance of the communications, her telephone, otherwise mouth, is never shut. She talks from morning til night, and all night and next day! And she is quite extensively as married as she is otherwise burdened with care. To her certain knowledge she has been married seventeen times, and is the anxious mother of two hundred and fifty children of her own, besides a whole lot of stepchildren and grand-children. As a consequence every single person who come "singly or in battalions" through the wards are taken right into her motherly old heart, as one of hers, or her husband's, or her son's son, or one of her step-daughter's children, for in every single instance she discovers some family resemblance whereby she can claim them. She says, "Agnew Chafey," as she calls me, is about the sassyest child she ever had, and accounts for it by saying she had not the raising of me, since my father took me away from her when I was quite young.

But she generally adds, dear old lady: "But, Agnew, you have some real good streaks about you after all, and your bark's always worse than your bite!" I said once to her: "Auntie, where are all your husbands?" "Well," she answered, with a merry twinkle of her pretty blue eyes, "I left some of them and some of them left me, and the Lord took some of them!" Think of that will you! Some of them! She is so perfectly sincere in her "delusions" and so contented and happy, too, that one can scarcely realize when in her presence how sad also her case is. She is cheerful and bright all the time, and only once in a while needs calling to order and then her anger is terrible. That "young snips of girls" should attempt to control her! One morning in the early spring she was so busy eating her breakfast, in order to get through soon, that she forgot to talk, and in a few moments asked to be excused, and after the "ladies" were dismissed from the dining-room one of the attendants went into the bath-room and there was the "Ruler Extraordinary," with sleeves rolled up, washing ward blankets! Old house-keeping associations were too strong to be easily broken! The traditions of her many spring house cleanings were revived, and washing blankets naturally occurred to her as a preliminary. She had already about half a dozen soaped and soaking in boiling water in the bath tub, and when the girls fished them out and threw them "down the shute" she was furious in her anger. Dear old Auntie! What a tender affectionate heart you ha! And yet ever one teased her so! Once after my recovery I was going into Indianapolis for the day, and as I was leaving the ward she said: "Look here, Agnew, where are you gadding to now?" And I said I am going down to Greensburg, her former home. Have you any message to send, and she said pleasantly: "Tell everybody I'm well." We did not meet again until next morning at breakfast, where we occupy the same table, she at the head and I at the foot. After we were seated, she said; "Well, did you see any of my folks?" And I said: "I went all through, that town and only saw one man — a poor miserable, bow-legged, slab-sided, knock-kneed, rickety sort of an individual," and I asked him if he knew the Widow H, who used to live there. "Know her," he said, "I think I do! I'm the only man in this town she didn't marry, and she'd a had me certain only I had her put in the insane asylum in pure self-defense!" I wish I could describe her contemptuous tone, as she said, after giving me the contents of her coffee-cup for my sass. "I know very well who that was, the infernal old liar, it sounds just like him, and I never wanted to marry him!" Not a single doubt of my veracity, but her indignation was aroused from the ridicule implied, and no one was more sensitive to ridicule than she, even tho' so insane. Months before, when in my hatred of myself and all mankind, including particularly womankind, I used to drive her and her everlasting telephone away from my end of the hall — not at all particular as to my language. She would say: "Why, my goodness gracious, master, do hush! Why, honey, don't you know its just perfectly outrageous the way you swear! You just shut right straight up now, or I'll box your ears — see if I don't! You never got that from me! I'm afraid old Bill Chafey wasn't any too particular in your bringing up." There it was again! I never got any badness of mine from any body! At least no body was ever willing to shoulder any fault of mine, or help me bear it. I reckon, like "Topsy," "I just growed."

CHAPTER XVII.

It is true
That we have wept, but oh, this thread of gold!
We would not have it tarnished, let us turn
Oft and look back upon the wondrous web,
And when it shineth, sometimes, we may know,
That memory is possession. — Jean Ingelow.

My readers will understand that these extracts were from
letters written at different stages of my convalescence, and
some of them after I was comparatively well. At the first stage
of my improvement, after having conquered my craving for
chloral, I was weaker than a child in my lack of self-control. A
word, a look of sympathy would bring the quick tears. Often
the doctor, in passing, would lay his hand on my head a
moment, or touch my hand, and these simple little marks of
interest, when omitted, positively hurt me. But as I slowly, but
surely improved, the time came when I did not care to be
treated as a baby, and as a consequence, almost perceptibly,
his manner changed toward me also, and I was treated as a
reasonable woman again. One morning our supervisoress
came in my room with a bundle, saying, "Here is a present for
you from the doctor;" and opening it, spread upon the floor a
beautiful Brussels rug. I never was so surprised and delighted!
and she stood there enjoying my expressions of wonder, that
any one should be so kind to me! almost crying herself
through sympathy. When the doctor came in an hour or so
later, I was sitting on that rug down on the floor, a very child
in my admiration of its beautiful figures and texture. And
after thanking him as coherently as I could under the
surprising circumstances, I asked him if he had ever read of
the man who became a bankrupt through the buying a pair of
brass andirons? He said he had not and, I advised him to hunt
it up, but at the same time I warned him that I should keep my

rug. I have spoken of my intense love of music! There were
times at the beginning of my convalescence of almost
desperation! Feelings of intense excitement, of which I was
compelled to give utterance to of some sort. If there was a
chair or any thing within my reach that I could break, or
failing in that, a window through which I could dash my
hand, and if blood came, all the better, the paroxysm would
soon pass over. Heretofore, such relief had been obtained by
swearing, horribly swearing too, though sometimes inaudibly.
But the time came, when I reasoned thus: I ought not to swear!
I did not use to! Not that I think so called profanity very
sinful, but it's not refined. Ladies as a general thing don't
swear, and I won't any more! But these desperate feelings,
what should I do? for they would come, and I would listen to
the piano and wish. Oh! so earnestly, that I dared just to try if
I could recall some of my old songs "I sung long years ago,
since they were unforgotten still, and sadly dear to me—I'd
try to sing those old songs, they were so sweet to me!" And
one evening, just at twilight, when I knew my regular
attendants were absent and the "detail," a stranger to me and
my past, I went to the piano, and though my fingers were so
nervous from weakness and emotion, that I could scarcely
strike the chords; I did strike them, and I sang,

> "Joys that we've tasted
> May some times return,
> But the torch when once wasted,
> Oh! how can it burn?"

and I sang "Oft in the Stilly Night," and "Then You'll
Remember Me," and others of the dear old songs, sweeter and
purer than any of the new ones, until a feeling almost of peace
came to my troubled heart. Blessed music! While singing, the
patients gathered around me perfectly amazed, and quietly
the door of the attendant's room opened, and some body's
arms were around me and a kind voice said brokenly, "Oh, I
am so glad! Do you know I believe you are going to get well

now, right straight along! Why, I never dreamed you could play!" It was one of our "night watches," the one who gave me the last dose of "night medicine" I ever took. I remember once she said to me when I was "in the depths," "Mrs. Agnew, why won't you allow persons who are so inclined, to be kind to you? I know I want to treat you kindly if you would let me;" and I answered, "Oh, you be damned." I don't believe though, that I ever swore or felt the slightest inclination to swear after I began singing; there was no longer the necessity for such expression for over-wrought feeling; music had supplied the want; and in the twilight, oftener than at any other hour, I sang, since at that hour I most frequently recalled the past, and drank over again from my sadly mixed cup of fate, sweet and bitter memories. Then truly could I appreciate the tenderness of the sentiment contained in the following bit of poetry sent me by one who sympathized with and understood my loneliness:

> "When a silence comes upon me with the closing of the day,
> When the volume, all unheeded, from my fingers slips away,
> When the last faint smile of sunset has faded from the pane,
> The present passes with it, and the past comes back again.
>
> And through the gathering darkness, I see faces dear and fair.
> The quick, uncertain childish steps are sounding on the stair,
> Warm hands, once folded cold and still, are clasping me again.
> And tender, long hushed voices, call the name familiar then.

The loneliness, the doubting, the silence of long years,
The days of weary yearning, the nights of bitter tears.
The failures after efforts, the trustfulness betrayed,
The resignation, bitter sweet for joys too long delayed.

All these fall from me, and once more before me lies my
life.
Once more I taste the sweet, false dream that comes
before the strife.
Once more love, faith and constancy are something
more than name.
And castles, fair and noble, my vivid fancy frames.

Ah! well, 'tis but a moment that I hold them to my
heart,
And search each face with eager eyes, so long we are
apart,
'Tis but for one short moment, yet I know they are
unchanged,
Those dear dead ones who loved me can never be
estranged!"

And not only was my music a comfort to me, it was also
entertainment for the unfortunates around me, and many a
curious concert we held, as one and another would call for
some favorite song or hymn, as an encouragement to me in
my efforts to pick out a suitable accompaniment, that "they
would help me sing." Once I remember "Aunt Betty" saying,
"Do sing 'When I can read my title clear to mansions in the
skies;'" and I said, "But I didn't read my title clear, 'Aunt
Betty,'" and she answered, "Well, sing it any way, for I do
thank the Lord!" and as I began singing, and several others
joined me in the chorus, "We will stand the storm, and we'll
anchor bye-and-bye," she began shaking hands with others
gathered around and crying "Glory! glory!" in regular
Methodist camp-meeting style, until the excitement became

contagious, as all religious excitements do, and one young
girl, an excellent elocutionist mounted a table, and began an
exhortation, partly in fun and partly in earnest; another one
turned down several chairs in a 'sort of circle' around the
piano improvising a mourner's bench, and began calling upon
sinners to "come forward and be prayed for," and through it
all rang the "choir" screaming out "We will stand the storm;"
and storm it was, and such a "revival of religion" was
inaugurated on the old "fourth ward," as to require quite a
force of the authorities to quell it. And who dares say there
was not quite as much religion in that revival as many similar
manifestations "outside the bars," and no more levity than is
expressed by some of the *pious* utterances of so-called
evangelists of the present day. When the doctor heard of it, he
said gravely, "Did you start all that hub-bub last night? I'm
surprised at you!"

> Better trust all and be deceived,
> And mourn that trust, and that deceiving,
> Than doubt one word, which if believed,
> Had blessed thy soul, with true believing. — Whittier.

CHAPTER XVIII.

I THINK I can give my readers no better proof of the improvement of one year in my mental condition than by reproducing a letter to a former dear friend, one who had been particularly kind to me during a severe illness of myself and little child.

Insane Asylum,

Thanksgiving Day, 1884.

I presume you will be surprised, though I trust not unpleasantly so, to receive a letter from me. Among the many I am thinking of to-day, you are prominent; and I can not but contrast my present feelings and surroundings with one year ago; I was only just beginning then to improve, and that morning when the doctor made his usual morning round and asked, "Does not this bright beautiful morning make you feel more cheerful?" saying "it should do so;" I could not answer in the affirmative; I had given no thought to the day; whether the sun shone or the rain fell, mattered but little to me—and feeling I had nothing to be thankful for. "Thanksgiving day" was to me a dead letter. If you could only come into my room this morning, you have no idea what that little visit of yours a year ago, was to me, and I can't put it into words. I wrote to my sister that it was as though a ray of sunshine had fallen upon a dark cloud, because I felt that your visit was not from morbid curiosity; I felt you were my friend, and I had so few of them; and yet I sat there almost silent, and could not tell you I was glad—could not tell you, Mrs. M., not that I did not wish to talk to you. This has been a peculiar feature of my mental trouble, that up to within some thing over a year, I had not the power, even after I had the faculty of thought—of continued intelligent thought—of clothing my thoughts in language, I seemed not to have any words. I want you to say

this to Dr. Charlton for me; when he and Mrs. C. were here
last to see me—though by Dr. Rogers' countenance I presume
since he was with them—they took an ungenerous advantage
of my helplessness by walking in upon me abruptly; I would
have been only too glad if I could have said to them what was
in my heart to say; Dr. Charlton as a physician should have
known so, and as a Christian, and my trusted physician, in
more than one time of trial, should not have so misjudged me,
whose burden was already too heavy to bear. When you were
leaving me, do you remember you said, "Do not think of the
bad but think of our good Lord?" I am not a bad woman, Mrs.
M.; I didn't think I ever was a willfully bad person; I used to
think when we were friends, that I was tolerably good; I know
I tried to be. But several years ago this "Good Lord" in his
infinite mercy, loving kindness and tender compassion, saw
fit to consign me to the only hell I am ever afraid of being
again sent to—insanity; and alone, unaided and unfriended, I
struggled and fought my way out in spite of the devils within
my own soul and surrounding me, in the shape of humanity.
So if it was a battle, and a fearful one, the good elements of my
nature triumphed, and this day is to me truly a Thanksgiving,
for restored bodily strength, and, as a consequence,
strengthened mind to enable me to meet whatever the future
holds for me, and to successfully refute the unjust charges that
have been brought against me, of unfulfilled duty and "willful
neglect of my family" in the past. I am thankful for this
home—I love to call this place an asylum—and right here,
where under Dr. Walker, I had worse than brutal treatment,
and that too, at a time when I was raving mad, therefore
helpless—I claim now scores of friends, upon whom I can
rely. The Lord never put breath into a meaner thing than that
man, I reckon; the Lord made him—at least when there was
no more dirty work for him to do—as a compensation to
nature, for such an outrage upon her laws, he killed him. I
presume just such an instrument was necessary to carry out
certain "designs" against me, as there were men among them,

who remembering there was a poor, helpless woman to be tortured, feared their hearts might falter as they thought of their wife and mother, before the miserably planned work was complete; but he died first, and I came slowly out of my hideous nightmare, and tried to breathe again. And let me tell you I had ready sympathy from the noble man who succeeded him. I shall never forget Dr. Thomas, for a kinder heart never beat in a grand big body; and through his influence, I was put under the skillful treatment and womanly tenderness of Dr. Sarah Stockton, since which time my improvement has been so rapid as almost to seem a miracle. I think Mrs. Fletcher the loveliest character I ever imagined. It requires only her presence in the wards to brighten the saddest face there. Dr. Fletcher is just himself, full of quiet humor, and overflowing with good works and kind attentions. They have a lovely family, and I am made to feel perfectly welcome in their apartments, as often as a change from the monotony of the ward is necessary or pleasant. Now, my dear friend, I am sure you will agree with me, that I have much to be thankful for, and be glad too, that I have this spirit; but at the same time you must know how very sad I am, considering my past, and anticipating my future. One hope sustains me. The time is coming when my children will think for themselves. They have bright minds. I hear from them from outside parties — actuated only by the purest humanity — and when that time comes, they will act independently, and will not believe their mother willfully left them to be cared for "through unexampled difficulty" by their father. What special merit should he claim for that? Who but the father should care for the children in the absence of the mother? I rejoice that they are boys, they will the more readily turn to their mother. While this hope is a comfort, I do not reproach myself with ever having in word, act or thought, been other than a faithful wife and mother, and in my affliction, most keenly have I felt that I was forsaken both by God and man. Now I would so much enjoy a letter from you; I remember every one of your family with affection. Say something kind to Mrs. E. for me; I am sure she felt I was glad to see her when she came here recently; and to all others who speak kindly of me, my regards.

Sincerely yours.

CHAPTER XIX.

My husband visited me for the last time Dec. 17, 1883, at which time I was confined to my bed, as was the case and had been periodically for several years, during which periods I suffered intensely, relief only being afforded by morphine administered by my physician. But at this stage of my convalescence I was able to relieve the monotony somewhat by reading, and had at the time on my bed a book on biology, in which I told him I was deeply interested. He looked at it and said, "What sort of thing is it?" And I answered: "You will understand that better after you read it." "Oh," he answered, "I have no time to read for the cultivation of my intellect. My 'time' is employed solely in getting bread and butter for 'my children.'" He has persistently claimed an exclusive ownership in our children, and I told him he should certainly take out a "patent on that right" as something a little out of the ordinary. He would not probably be disturbed in his monopoly by infringement, and I told him later in a letter, after he had thrown off all disguises and clearly "shown his hand," that my most charitable conclusion concerning him was that he was insane, and that in the probable event of his "coming to himself" behind the bars, I would advise him to devote his abundance of surplus time to the study of heredity, not exclusively, that of insanity! There are worse taints! he would find then he had no scarcity of time; but a disgusting superfluity of time! Time would be about all he would have, and probably he might become so wearied with its intolerable plenty as to try ineffectually, as did his wife, to get away from Time and all that pertains thereto, by getting out of the world I It was in this same letter, I think, that occurred this oft repeated, much quoted "insulting" sentence: "Penitence is a virtue I do not cultivate." Penitence undoubtedly was intended to read Patience. However, I am not at all particular that it should be corrected, since penitence implies recognized, acknowledged guilt, and this I must emphatically deny. He spent a portion of the afternoon with me, and during the time I insisted that he should read a number of letters written me by my sister, in which she urged me to keep up good heart and I would soon be able to go home to my family. He said, "You seem from these replies to have written very freely to your sister." And as he was leaving he said: "I reckon you won't write to me!" One month later, after having had special treatment and close attention from Dr. Sarah Stockton, and finding myself greatly improved, I wrote him quite a lengthy letter, wrote just as kindly as I felt. Told him how much better I was, and how encouraged I felt at the prospect of getting well, and at the close asked him particularly to send me his and the childrens' pictures. Then, more because he had been very profuse in his offers to send me any thing I needed than that I positively needed the things, since the state furnishes patients those necessaries, I asked him to send me a good pair of glasses and some postage stamps. This letter I did not keep a copy of! I was writing to my husband and did not consider it necessary. I am wiser since. Within three days his answer came! A scrap of blank paper, inclosing twenty-eight cents in postage stamps, in a sealed envelope directed to me! I immediately returned him a note for the same amount of stamps, "payable to him or his order one day after date!" and within a month was out of his debt! And the battle had opened between us!

> "Beware of entrance to a quarrel, but being in
> Bear 't that the opposed may beware of thee." —
> Shakespeare.

CHAPTER XX.

> Friend is a word of loyal tone —
> Friend is a poem, all alone. — George Elliot.

I don't think my sisters of the woman's rights party will care to claim me as one of them. Indeed I doubt very much if I understand what they really wish in the matter of rights any better than the majority of them do themselves. I've had a sufficiency of female sufferage! And not having any property need not concern myself about the justice or injustice of taxation without representation, or make any exertion to understand the difference between misrepresentation and taxation. There now! I'm all mixed up! I knew I would be if I attempted deep water in my little boat! Won't some of my learned sisters straighten me out? Of course there would be considerable condescension in the attempt to give this aid to an humble tho' aspiring sister. Hours of "innocuous desuetude" might, however, be more appropriately employed so than in the presuming of attempting a written criticism upon George Elliot, whose writings are in themselves sermons. I won't venture a single idea upon civil or uncivil service or the tariff, but upon one reform — of woman — I do with all my soul sanction her education as a physician! And for the sake, and in behalf of suffering woman — insane women in particular — since they can not tell their misery, I make an appeal to the board of trustees of every female hospital for the insane in the land, for the appointment of a woman upon their medical staff. I often tell my dear friend, Dr. Stockton, that I still think her a handsome woman! But I felt the first time she came into my darkened room, where I lay in such agony as only miserable women suffer, and seating herself at my bedside, looking pityingly at me, the expression in her lovely blue eyes in itself a mute promise of assistance, before a word was spoken, that an angel had been with me.

Am I too enthusiastic? If I could only express the hopefulness her words inspired, not that I cared then to live, for I did not, but I was so thankful to be relieved from my terrible physical sufferings, and she was so handsomely dressed, too! And such lovely diamonds! And as I had a woman's admiration for lovely things and only a child's self control, I immediately began appropriating her rings, which she seemed not to notice. So, for a few brief moments, I was the happy possessor of life-long, coveted diamonds! And I still retain my admiration for my friend, and have added to my admiration of her personal appearance and intellectual endowments — love — for her never failing kindness and sympathy toward me in my sorrowful life. Thus this advantage one possesses in having a woman for your physician. If you love her you can tell her so. In the other sex you must tell his wife how much you think of her husband, and that's a satisfaction, too, when you also love the wife, since there's not that woman lives who does not like to hear nice things said of her husband. It is indirectly a delicate compliment to her good taste, since she chose him, or was chosen by him. I remember once when quite a young girl my brother, who was a physician, ten years older than myself, found me one day in his private office pouring over a medical work, and taking the volume out of my hand said, "Are you reading this heavy matter merely through curiosity, or are you really interested in it?" And I told him I was deeply interested and wished I might study the profession of medicine. "Well," he replied, "If you were a man I would take you for a student!" Before his death, which was of recent date, he was in entire sympathy with reform in this direction, and heartily indorsed my enthusiasm, and honored me for my freely expressed affection for my individual doctor, and entered fully into my feeling of regret that I were not twenty years younger that I might yet study this the grandest of the professions.

After my complete recovery, during the year in which I was in a measure the "guest of the State of Indiana," I was allowed free access to several fine medical libraries, also had permission to read valuable authorities on points of especial interest to me; thus learning much that it were well all parents could know familiarly. And in reading, I remembered with pain, how often in the past I had, after maneuvering vainly not to get him "started," as he himself expressed it, tried to make my little son stop crying when he wanted, "Oh, he just wanted to cry! Oh, so awful, mamma!" lie seemed not to be able to understand why he should not be allowed to cry it out! Dear little Kye! I'll shoulder that "streak!" He is his mamma's own boy! And in every brutal effort at "breaking my will" my precious little high-tempered reliable boy came before me almost like a ghost. A valued friend said to me once when speaking of his peculiar temperament, "'Don't you worry about that boy being bad; he is too smart to make a bad man!" And the little chap heard him and took advantage of it the next time he needed correction, by saying, "Well, mamma, if I'm bad I'm too smart to be a berry bad man!" and I don't worry any more! It is an ever present trouble that I am deprived of the precious privilege of watching those boys develop into manhood, but some of their childish utterances stay with me and comfort me as tho' they were words of sacred prophecy.

During my early affliction, while yet at home, I felt terribly that probably my children might be taunted by unthinking persons over my condition, and one day when there were no one else present but my two eldest boys I said to the eldest one, "Do they ever say at school that your mamma is crazy?" He gave me a troubled look, but before he could reply the other one, my little "West Point Cadet" as he hopes to be, sprang up with flashing eyes and clenched fist and said, "Yes, sir, mamma, yes, sir! one boy did say that to Dadie, and Dadie! he just up with a darnick and let him have it right on the head, sir!" Quite a supply of boyish slang in the recital I admit, but is there not also nobility of character, and may I not expect and hope for manly support and sympathy from such boys, some time yet? In my reading, painful facts of heredity were made plain — mysterious, touchy points, sore spots of domestic history were understood, of which, thank heaven, I am free! I can afford to be, and am not at all sensitive regarding pedigree, since there's nothing to evade! No "black drop" to fear or guard against! And this study of heredity, though a painful one at times, should teach us to be charitable in our judgment of the faults of others, since they may be victims of taints, coming down through generations.

Persons in general can have no idea of the warm personal attachments formed among this unfortunate class. Once during my second year in the asylum an old German woman on our ward was reported at the point of death, and upon no account was she to be given water to drink. She had been one of the silent sort, too, scarcely ever speaking to any one, but as I went into her room just at twilight she said, "Oh good lady, shust one drink, for God's sake!" I said, "Mrs. C. they say water will kill you!" "No, no," she cried, "I will die without." And so I made her promise not to tell and gave her a tin cupful. She drank as tho' famished, and sank back on her pillow gasping so goot, so so goot, so goot! The next morning her bed was vacant. And I did not know until four years after but that my cup of water killed her.

One day after having attained to the dignity of a "trusty," having "keys of my own, I thank you," I was going through the other division from ours when some one caught me around the neck, crying "The good laty, I not forget, I not forget, I never vill!" and there was my dead old friend, bright as a lark! The happiest old lady in the ward! But alas! never to come from "under her cloud!" Yet she did not forget the cup of cold water given in violation of the rules! Think you the "recording angel," if such there be, forgot to put that on my credit side? My conscience never had condemned me for the act. The influence of my christian traditions, when I read the bible in faith, were strong yet within me, and I remember another one, "who in hell lifted up his voice and begged if only but one drop to cool his parched tongue." Was I wrong?

CHAPTER XXI.

> There are inscriptions upon our hearts, which like those upon "Deighton Rock" are never seen, excepting at dead low ebb. — O. W. Holmes.

My sister got all my secrets those days without pumping for them, simply by her unceasing kindness to me, and it was a relief to me after my years of painful repression to give free vent to my feelings. Before the Christmas holidays of 1883, she sent me a box of presents, both for comfort and adornment, among which was a lovely white apron. The week following New Year s day I wrote, "I must tell you what a wonderful metamorphosis your present of a white apron made. I could not, of course, put on that lovely thing over one of my shabby well-worn calico gowns, and I had sworn in my wrath, that I never would wear any other sort unless I paid for it myself Since — were you aware — that until after I had become Madam, I never had worn any thing better than calico? Are you aware of this fact? I was quite surprised myself to learn this, but as one of the members of the 'unspotted (?) old Irish Presbyterian family,' of which I became a member by marriage, says so, I must accept it as a fact, and the contrary belief held by me for so many years, must simply stow itself away among a number of other exploded 'delusions.' Fortunately, though, for those who desired to see 'that awful looking Mrs. Agnew' in something better than calico, there remained one single garment of my former married splendor, a black cashmere dress; one I had traveled in up to the Lunatic Asylum. I had never worn it since, but had begged my attendants, at different times (in vain), to give the thing away to some one more accustomed to wearing good clothing than myself, or to throw it down the 'rag-shute;' but no, they held on to that everlasting old cashmere like grim death, and so the historical old dud — for it has a history if I had the patience to go into particulars — was well shaken before being taken, and put on New Year's day, and as I held it up between me and the light, I congratulated myself that in consequence of the frequent raids of moth and mice during five years, it might also serve me for summer wear, and to the uninitiated might pass for a grenadine. Well, the dress and apron called loudly for something white about the neck, and again a relic of my extensive married wardrobe made its appearance in the form of a little ruching, which I put on, and I declare I began to feel so sort of nice, and natural too, as though in some former state I might have been somebody, or at least *somebody's wife*, I really could not stay all alone in my glory in my own room, so I walked out on the hall, and calmly (?) waited for compliments. Several evenings after I 'dressed up' again, and was seated at a table playing 'backgammon' with one of my friends — a patient — when the doctor came in and said, 'That is positively an act of charity, teaching these poor women that interesting game; and now, won't you come down to-morrow and spend the afternoon with me in my office?' and I answered, 'No, sir, certainly not!' 'Why not?' he asked, and I said, 'Because I don't think I should feel at all comfortable doing go;' and he said, 'Oh, nonsense! Now you think the matter over and do come;' and after thinking it over I concluded I would accept the invitation, and so I again entered society. After my attendant, who accompanied me to the office door, left me, I think for some moments I did not exactly know 'where the land lay,' but the bright room, handsome carpet, pretty furniture, and above all, the suggestive book-cases, together with the glowing coal fire in the open grate looking so home like, I was soon at my ease and thoroughly enjoyed my 'afternoon out,' and carried home with me my arm full of never failing — though mute friends — good books." Not long after this letter was written, I also formed the acquaintance of the doctor's wife, and another constant friendship was formed, and additional means of enjoyment offered me, since her music was a constant feast to me, listening to her lovely voice as she patiently sang one after another of her own and my favorites. Often I was drawn away from my own immediate sorrow as much as was possible. I have yet to hear Mrs. Dr. Thomas speak an unkind or uncharitable word of any one, and a year or more later, as I was bidding her good-bye, before starting upon the uncertain visit to my children, she said as she held my hand, "I am sorry you have not more faith in prayer, but you can't help my prayers for you, and every breath will be a prayer for you and your children while you are away from us."

I was almost wild when the conclusion was forced upon me, that if I ever was to see my children again, I must go there myself I had before this, gone in anguish of heart, to Dr. Fletcher, begging—since I had no rights under the law while still a patient—for my discharge, so as to be put on a legal footing to fight that man. First of all to see my children and learn from them, if, as their father said, I was forgotten. And when he said, after my appeal to him, "In Heaven's name, have you no friends, no relatives, who will give you the protection of their home while you fight for your rights?" I said, "I will not accept the charity of any relative I have. Yes, I have plenty of such, but after having been independent in my own home, I will not become a dependent upon any one, however closely related, but I will gladly work here; I have strong hands, and willing and determined heart, and will do any thing; go into your kitchen, any place, only give me my discharge;" and he said, "Mrs. Agnew, I would as freely give you my hand and seat you at my table as any lady of my acquaintance, if it were my own table, but you shall have your discharge, and I will give you all the assistance within my power, until you feel there is some other place where you are willing to go."

CHAPTER XXII.

"No earnest work
Of any honest creature, how be't weak,
Imperfect, ill adapted, fails so much.
It is not gathered, as a grain of sand,
For carrying out God's ends." — Elizabeth Browning.

Through the thoughtfulness of Dr. Thomas, arrangements
were made for my employment in the sewing room, the
trustees agreeing to pay me a small sum monthly, dating from
March 5, 1884, and continuing until my discharge, April 21,
1885. It was a great relief from the monotony of ward life, and
the money, too, was very acceptably received, and though I
was only expected to spend a part of the day serving, I gave
my whole time exclusively to my work; I had been a
pensioner — upon the bounty of the State — for so many years,
that I felt it my duty to make all the return in my power; at the
same time, each "pay day," I drew my little allowance very
cheerfully, and spent my first month's pay in some little
articles for my children, but was positively, and most
peremptorily forbidden by my husband to send them, since
using his own language, "I will not allow them to receive any
thing from you, neither will I allow them to be reminded that
you still live; let them forget your last days spent with them if
they can! Let them forget if they can!" and in reply I wrote,
"Have you forgotten the three days previous to the last day
spent with them, and the entertainment gotten up by you,
their father, for the benefit of your sister? A little seven year
old boy knocked down by your fist and dragged screaming
into an adjoining room, where, after the key was turned upon
me, his insane mother, he was ordered to strip off his coat 'and
get down upon his knees,' when he was whipped like a dog,
with a leather strap, I, in the meantime being entertained by
language such as I had not then thought could pass a woman's

lips, and which I still think unsurpassed in vileness by any insane raving heard since. What was his offense? Simply because that little child had, with his brother — still younger — gone down town to see "Barnum's circus" come in, instead of going (as good little Christians following in the footsteps of their pious paternal ancestors) to Sunday-school. Another "streak" I'll pick up, and own willingly. I remember very distinctly, years since, when a whole lot of little girls, I among the number, prominently too, I presume, since I was generally the leader in all sorts of mischief, ran off from school and crawled in under the canvas because we did so want to see the circus, and we hadn't any money, and our parents wouldn't probably allow us to go if we were to ask permission, and besides "stolen fruit was ever so sweet." I well remember when the clown, getting a glimpse of half a dozen or more scared little faces under the seats, gave a yell that frightened us out of a year's growth, but the kind-hearted manager invited us out and gave us front seats — "reserved seats" — for deserving little girls, who had aspirations above *just* school. The last summer I spent at the asylum I attended another circus. Forepaugh was in Indianapolis, and Dr. Fletcher arranged for a "circus party," that, I am sure, has no precedent in any other asylum. I was entirely well, but was invited to go with the party; a special street car was chartered, and the party, consisting of twelve insane women. Dr. Fletcher — our gentlemanly druggist — and four attendants, besides myself, started in town, three miles distant, to attend the evening exhibition. Reserved seats had been provided, and all went smoothly; one old German lady, as we readied the ground, seemed in danger of becoming separated from the crowd, and our "drug store man," as she called him, went to help her along, when she cried out so as to attract attention, "Sthop now, Got in himmel! Shust you look after some old beobles, and let young beoples pe, I shust dinks Dr. Fletcher pe pretty vell known here, and if I gets lost, I say I shust be one of his kinder, by golly!" She was over seventy years of age; but very soon we were quietly seated, and the doctor remarked that he did not think his crowd presented any thing of an unusual appearance, any more than many other crowds of the same size; they were all nice looking and quiet. I said, "But Doctor, suppose it was announced in this quiet tent, that one dozen 'lunatics from the asylum' were here in a crowd, don't you imagine there would be more reserved seats vacated suddenly than would be filled again to-night?" and he said, "How would it do to have a jolly good performance of our own after the regular programme is gone through?" and he had not long to wait before "our own performance" began; I think the doctor must have supplied himself liberally with small change before he started, but I imagine several bills also were exchanged before the scenes closed. "Our crowd" completely monopolized the "ice cold lemonade," pop-corn and "candy" stock, but the fun reached the screaming point when the pea-nut man began calling out his delicious wares, "Here's your fresh roasted pea-nuts, just out of the hopper." Now my uninitiated friend you are not obliged to laugh, since you don't understand the significance of the "hopper" in hospital parlance; you might not have considered it so excruciatingly funny as we did, when one of our party sang out, "Just out of the hopper, well I'll be damned! go to hell with your damned old pea-nuts just out of the hopper!" and when Dr. Fletcher, pressing his arm around her, said, "You be still, Laura," she said, "That's all right, Doctor, give me another squeeze, it's been a devilish long time since I've had a man's arm around me!" I am sure no one in that "circus party" will ever forget that night, and I think the doctor was fully convinced of the ability of his crowd in the way of performance, independent of programme, or precedents, so my readers will understand that gloom does not universally prevail among the insane, and in our institution nothing that can in any way add to the comfort or enjoyment of the inmates is considered too difficult to attempt. A school is a recent innovation upon usual methods among this class, and it is surprising how many elderly women gladly embrace this, their first opportunity of learning to read, to say nothing of other branches taught. Many of the inmates are already experts with the needle, and gladly add to their knowledge of plain sewing, all sorts of fancy stitches, and in consequence there is a very creditable display of some times really beautiful articles, ticketed for sale in the reception room, and in this way, not only are the patients complimented by having their work appreciated, but quite a sum is by this means returned to the hospital treasury. Each ward is also supplied with some sort of musical instrument, either a piano or organ, and books, flowers and pictures add their refining, softening influence to the home-like appearance. Our chapel, or amusement hall, either, as it was used for both religious services and dancing, was the pride of the whole house, and among those who at all realized what fire and danger meant, I don't think there was one dry eye when that beautiful room was wrapped in flames, and it was sadly realized that the brave firemen battled in vain in its defense. I remember well the night it was dedicated, as Dr. Fletcher said to fun, crowded with employes, of which, in the different departments there are several hundred, he called upon them all to pledge him their support in his effort to ameliorate as far as possible the gloom of tho unfortunates under his charge, and right nobly they responded, with cheer after cheer, for Dr. Fletcher, as he, leading his wife out upon the floor, opened the ball, playfully compelling her to go through the "quadrille," spite of her protestations that she "could not dance."

CHAPTER XXIII.

Lose this day loitering 'twill be the same story
To-morrow, and the rest more dillatory.
Thus indecision brings its own delays,
And days are lost lamenting over days. — Goethe.

The sewing-room of the institution is esteemed an oasis in
their otherwise monotonous life. It is a large room on the
fourth floor, extending over the entire center building, and its
high ceiling and immense windows make it a splendid and
cheerful looking room. There are a number of regularly
employed sewing girls under the supervision of a forewoman,
and it is wonderful the amount of sewing that is. done there
monthly. Dresses, as one item, running up well into the
hundreds, and all other garments worn by women in the same
proportion, besides the regular weekly or monthly
requisitions of the ward and official departments of bedding,
towels, napkins and tablecloths, including also curtains
necessary, all through this large building. The patients are
divided into two classes — home supplied and state or county
patients — and many of the friends of those supplied at home
prefer to furnish the material and have themselves charged
with the making by the state. So one may imagine the
hundreds of yards of material used there monthly. Going to
the sewing-room to assist is not obligatory upon any patient.
But the messenger from there at 9 A. M. very rarely opens the
door of any ward, and calls "ladies for the sewing-room"
without a ready response from some half a dozen or more
anxious to get to work. And soon after nine a wonderful big
"sewing bee" is in full swing. Imagine, if you can, such a
clatter of tongues! For woman will talk, sane or insane, and
busy fingers as well as tongues fly, and occasionally some
singer (?) will tune up and numerous others will join in, each

singing her own particular tune, or no tune at all, and some body else will for variety swear until the atmosphere is blue, while over there in the "patching corner" several old cronies are enjoying a choice "dish of gossip," discussing their "ward secrets" that they have been cautioned strictly by their attendants not to tell at the sewing-room, but which they invariably do tell, very much after the manner of their sane sisters. And so the wonderful machine moves on day after day, smoothly, as well regulated works always do when the "master mechanic" is at the same time kind hearted, as well as level-headed. The sewing-room, from its importance to the institution on account of its work, also as being an important curative factor in the treatment of the insane, since by this means their thoughts are directed from themselves, thus inducing forgetfulness of personal sorrow, by giving employment to their hands, is a special pride of our administration, and a special point of interest to which the attention of visitors is directed, and said visitors are more frequently treated to unexpected exhibitions here than in any other department in the building. The same old German lady, of circus fame, makes it a point to be present one half of each day, and particularly at such times when advertised "excursions" are expected to make a raid upon the insane asylum, and it is wonderful how such news does fly through the wards, reminding one of certain small country towns, where every body's private affairs are of public interest and attentively attended to. This old auntie "Sophia," as she calls herself, wears out on an average one pair of shoes each month "at the state's expense, by Got," but on such "state occasions" she will select the shabbiest old pair of slippers she has herself or can borrow, and as a crowd of gaping sightseers are engineered into the large room, she will go bobbing up to them with, "Goot morning, shentlemens and laties, you will like to see von 'Groos-mutter' valtz a little?" And as she chases before them, with her little soft white curls and wrinkled old face, they laugh and say: "Oh, certainly, grandmother," "if you can valtz, we would be delighted to see you." If she can! I wish you could see her spinning around to her own music, sang or whistled. Many a ball-room belle might well envy her light, graceful step. But the surprise comes when she has finished. Up goes her apron and out slips her tattered slippers, as she says: "The shentlemans vill not let dis groos-mutter dance for nottings von she has so bad shoes, she shust must dance for money to puy so better vons as dese." Few care to risk her contemptuous expression, if they seemed not to be inclined to respond, and often her collections amount to quite a sum, for which she is profusely loud in her expressions of gratitude. Until their last footstep dies away in the distance, and then we are treated to a jig or double shuffle as she screams with laughter, saying: "Dam't-fools, come to see crazy people, eh? Vell all goot! You shust pay for dat all dat same!" Spend her money for shoes! Indeed, no! That money goes for sweetmeats and fruit, of which the old lady is extremely fond.

CHAPTER XXIV.

Oh wad some power the giftie gie us
To see ourselves as others see us
I wad fra many a blunder free us
And foolish notion. — Burns.

Could the general public, the different classes of which visit such institutions, with equally different motives, the professional sight seer, the philanthropist, the promiscuous excursion mob, or the select exclusive who occasionally honor (?) the inmates with a supercilious stare, know how frequently they are themselves outrageously duped by the "poor crazy creature" they have come to criticise, they might not feel so comfortable. Scarcely a day passes without some such unpremeditated unadvertised exhibition being given. Particularly during the many state anniversaries, fairs, conventions, and many others of like character, may such manifestations be expected and political campaigns furnish fun alive, both to patients and visitors. And I can assure you that politics is not only a subject of conversation there, but is read of and understood, and party distinctions and lines are quite as closely drawn and pronounced as those without, even tho' they do get terribly mixed over the candidates for the entertainment of some wise looking: statesman who laughs immoderately over such combinations as "Hurrah for Cleveland and Logan! I'm a St. John woman! By thunder!" Our "usher" during the last campaign had as much as she could do to keep from betraying to visitors that they were the victims and that the patient quite as often understood themselves and the platform upon which they stood as did the smiling voter so very much amused at their mixtures. Our attendants, too, all over the house, frequently play patient, generally hanging lovingly on to some dudish sort of a chap, whom they profess to recognize as some former lover, and several times quite touching scenes have been described by imaginative gushing reporters from some of our most reputable papers, said to have occurred on our insane wards. Such as: "When I entered the door I was immediately approached by a lovely young girl, with large mournful, soulful, blue eyes, in which smouldered the gloom of insanity, and with her wreath of golden hair disheveled and flowing, and a chill passed over me involuntarily as she said, oh, so mournfully, sinking on her knees, 'Please, kind sir, take me home with you?'" Dramatic, wasn't it? But that lovely creature was one of the attendants, up to that sort of thing, and her patients enjoyed seeing the reporter fooled quite as well as she.

During the last presidential campaign I had a large picture of our president hanging in my room, plainly visible to visitors passing through the ward. I was entirely well then, but still retained my room on the ward and sat there the greater part of the time sewing. My attendants and the usher told me they would hold themselves in readiness to at any time fall in with any joke I wished to play, and often visitors would stop at my door attracted by my candidate's picture, and would talk in subdued voices of the "quiet looking patient sitting there sewing so intently," and Alice — our usher — would say, with a sly mischievous look at me, "Yes, poor woman, she sits there most of her time generally quiet, but this fall she is greatly excited at times over politics, and is, as you see, a democrat, but she don't like folks to stare at her, so we had better move on." One day during September of '84 a gentleman came in alone with Alice, and just before reaching my room she gave a peculiar significant little ahem! and I heard her say, "oh Cleveland, of course! She has his picture. Just glance in as we pass, as she is excited to day, and at such times is considered dangerous." I sprang up, ran my hands through my short hair, which was just sufficiently curly, at that sort of treatment to stand "looking seven ways for Sunday" and was ready for inspection. He glanced in with a short merry ha! ha! So she is still a democrat? That speaks well for the democracy! and I recognized even by that slight glimpse a resemblance to Cleveland, and started on the jump after him! If you could have witnessed that race, down the short hall to the turn, which he rounded like a locomotive, then down the long hall to the door, out of which he sprang as the attendant, who ran ahead pretending to be terribly frightened for the man's safety, opened it. Just as he reached the door I struggled away from the "usher," who was pretending with the greatest difficulty to hold me, while she screamed to the brave (?) fellow, run, run! My goodness, man, don't let her catch you, and grabbed him by the coat collar, crying, no, sir! Grover you don't escape me this time! I've got you! The horrified expression in that man's eyes will never leave me as he looked back over his shoulders and sprang out into the hall, banging the door after him! Cleveland made a pretty good presidential race, but not to compare with his prototype trying toescape from a crazy admirer. The usher told me afterwards that when the door closed after him he stood there mopping the perspiration off his face and hands, and between gasps for breath said: "Good lord! I never was worse frightened! but really now, do yon suppose she really thought I was Grover Cleveland?" After having sufficiently recovered to proceed, Alice said, "Come on now, here are several more visiting wards." But he thanked her very kindly, saying, pointedly: "Not any more insanity for me!" Satisfied certainly of the soundness of my democracy, and I hope feeling sufficiently complimented, since he was mistaken for our president even by one "out of her mind."

Another time a party was going through, one of whom, a gentleman, carried a tempting looking basket of grapes, just then a rarity, and feeling inclined just then for some fun, also for some fruit, I walked up to the party, keeping step with them down the hall, and said just before reaching the door, "I want some grapes! Say, give me some grapes!" And a sweet looking young girl said, "Yes, auntie, you shall have a nice bunch, we will send you one after we go down stairs!" Send me some! I knew just how much that promise meant. Besides I had no intention of being adopted as every body's "auntie." So I said, "No you won't, my girlie! I want some grapes, and I want them now, and I want the whole basket full!" And the gentleman handed them over meek as a lamb, saying in an under tone to the young lady, "Never mind, dear, let the poor woman have them and I'll get you another basket in the city." Their secret was out! The same old story told again! I hope she is still "dear" to him, and earnestly hope their store of grapes and all other good things may never fail them, even tho' they were fooled out of probably his first married love token.

Once a party of exquisites of both sex were making the rounds of sights. A patient, not yet exactly sure of herself at all times, though possessed of a strong sense of the ludicrous, and of a fitness of things in general, said to one of the beaux of the crowd, who, with a lady upon his arm, was peering through eye-glasses, remarking upon the "wondah of this place, ah, say!" (at the same time looking anxiously in his face), "Haven't you made a mistake?" "Well no, madame, ah," he answered, "I think not, ah!" "Oh, yes you have, this isn't the home for feeble-minded, that's over at Nightstown, there's where you belong, poor fellow!" Persons who recognize these pictures — for they are facts — possibly won't care to be reminded of them, but certainly no one should blame- the inmates for retaliating as frequently as possible for impertinences of which they were the victims, before they were in a condition to resent, even much less retaliate such, (to them) insults. Visitors may well suspicion they are being victimized as often as they are treated to any thing unusual, in the way of "manifestation" on the part of the patients, since patients in reality "excited," are not on exhibition. There are days together when a visitor might stay upon some of our front wards and not discover any thing unusual, more than a number of plainly dressed, and sometimes queerly acting women, but as free from cranky notions, generally, as the same number in some neighborhoods outside; indeed I told Dr. Fletcher after my discharge, that I should go back home and bring him a whole car-load of people that I could spot as crazier than plenty of his present patients, but he begged so earnestly that I should not, that I promised him I would allow them to remain in blissful ignorance of their misery for his sake, since I can most heartily sympathize with the doctor, should he pray most earnestly to be delivered from any more patients from "our neighborhood," if in any particular they resemble me. I retained my room in the ward from choice almost a year after my recovery, and even yet I sometimes long for its crazy smallness. One friend after another added to my first article of civilization (my rug), articles both of use and ornament, until my little room of eight by fourteen was a bower of beauty. Think of my luxury! ruffled pillows, lace curtains surmounted by rep lambrequins, washstand and table, covered by pretty little scarfs; suppose they were merely "officer's towels" furnished me by the obliging housekeeper: everyone need not know one's little private economies. Ornaments in the shape of Japanese parasols and fans, a lovely hanging basket—through the kindness of our florist— several other pretty pictures besides our President's, and two rocking chairs, one for company, of which I had no scarcity, for I still continued the confidential friend of the majority of the patients, and I allowed them free access to my room when there myself, making but one single proviso, they were not to cry, I had enough of that sort of thing to do myself. One poor little woman, who did nothing else for about three months after she came, told me after her recovery, what a temptation my room used to be to her at times; that often she could scarcely restrain her impulse to rush in there and demolish every thing there, myself included, because I would not allow her to come to me with her everlasting "I want to go home!" I too, wanted with all my heart, to go home, and was in a condition to go, but my misery in this regard was not of a sort that loved company; we were good friends though through it all, and I helped her get ready to go home, when after only a few months' stay, her husband gladly came for her. Occasionally matters do not run altogether smoothly. Insane persons seem naturally suspicious, and generally are jealous, and the fact of me being presented at the time I began at the sewing-room, with a key to use at my discretion, was the means of my receiving one morning, when assisting my attendant with the morning work, a blow upon my head, by an iron mop stick in the hands of an infuriated "mistress of this house, I'll have you understand," that made the blood fly and laid me senseless for a few moments. I had just fitted my key in the lock of the clothing-room, when I heard, rather than felt the blow. Such things *will* sometimes occur and often give rise to sensational newspaper articles, of "patients in our insane asylum being allowed to batter the life out of each other, a state of affairs needing investigation," etc., etc. Patients do sometimes kill each other, and the attendants are not to blame, are at times powerless to prevent it, since it comes so suddenly; and it were well for the public to charitably reflect before deciding against the management of any such institution, since a very slight fire will, under encouraging circumstances, sometimes smoke considerably. It is the "ward secrets" hidden, particularly, and especially from the superintendent and physicians, that I am contending against, and I believe all honest officers of such institutions— and I have sufficient confidence in humanity to believe there are no others—will give my feeble efforts in this direction their hearty sanction. Below will be found my appeal to the Indiana Legislature, with the editor's remarks.

CHAPTER XXV.

A TOUCHING APPEAL.

We hope every member of the Indiana Legislature will read the article in to-day's "*Herald*," entitled, "Touching Appeal." The writer is a lady of unusual intelligence, who passed several years in the Indianapolis Asylum for the Insane, and was at last completely restored, as her strongly written appeal abundantly proves. The custom of admitting curiosity seekers into the institution had its origin in the suspicion of maltreatment, and is at last a reflection on the efficacy and probity of the asylum officials. It is as much as to say, if the people don't believe we are attending to our duties, let them come and see for themselves, and nine-tenths of the opened-mouthed starers who visit the institution have no interest beyond mere idle curiosity; a common phase of the milder forms of insanity is morbid sensitiveness, and the effect of being glowered at by strangers can not be better described than it is in the article of "*Non Compos Mentis*," who has felt it in all its accumulated terrors.

Editor.

To the Honorable Gentlemen of the Indiana Legislature:

It has been impressed upon my mind, since my discharge from the hospital for the insane—as a patient—that it is a duty I owe to humanity to make an appeal to the legislature for a law prohibiting the promiscuous visiting at that institution, and were it in my power to make you understand the positive torture many of those peculiarly unfortunate people suffer from the mere presence of the throngs of impertinent morbid curiosity seekers—from whom there is no escape in the wards of their prison—I am sure my attempt in their behalf will not be in vain. I use the word prison advisedly, and without intending the slightest reflections upon the management. "Bolts and bars" are but trifles compared with the mental torture endured by many of those miserable, self-convicted criminals, and suggest only the hope of rest and security from fancied (?) persecution. Poor afflicted victims! gathering a fearful harvest, not alone of their own sowing, tossed and tortured, and driven by a fate worse than death! Such, indeed, need an asylum, and such all institutions for the insane should be, and the "bolts and bars" that lock them and their terrible burden of misery within should assuredly lock without those who would curiously gaze upon without the slightest appreciation of their suffering the unhappy inmates. People are not insensible when insane, either to praise, censure or ridicule, and though I am far from charging all who visit the wards of the insane as being actuated by morbid curiosity, I do claim that there are but few exceptions among the inmates who do not resent such as intrusions; even the visits of relatives are not always a kindness. I know this in all its horrors; for three years almost I sat in one spot in the same old rocking chair, on the "fourth ward" of the hospital for the insane, fighting a battle with the Almighty, feeling I had no right to live, but not allowed to die, hoping and praying to choke to death at every bite I ate, yet forced to swallow food. Hating and cursing the sun that it shone and the flowers that they would bloom. A self-convicted criminal, answering at the judgment seat, my conscience, for every idle word or wicked thought, and yet as though my cup was not already full, I was outraged and tortured by the idle, unfeeling comments of careless people, sometimes strangers, often former friends, who I am sane, now, could not realize how they hurt me, but most frequently of persons whom I had formerly only known the existence of, who would not have dared presume to speak to, or of me before I "went crazy." Even now, in every nerve of my body, I realize the horror that seemed to take possession of my very soul as I would hear some one asking to see me, as a noisy crowd on "an excursion to Indianapolis," and bound to see the sights, was passing through the wards, and the answer of my attendant, "that's her settin' down there in the corner, but she's too mean to speak to any one, but go try her if you want to." At such times I have held up my poor helpless hands, and watched the "goose flesh" gather and stand upon my arms, and felt the cold chills creep over me as I waited and shivered in anticipation of the remarks sure to follow. "Can that be Mrs. Agnew?" "Don't she ever speak?" "Does she always sit there?" "Why, dear me, isn't it queer? she used to do so-and-so, and she used to be such-and-such!" and all I, poor miserable wretch, could do, was to wash the whole world — particularly the female world — had one neck and I had the power to strangle the life out of it. Oh, how bitterly I resented such cruelty, and I am sure mine is not an exceptional case in this respect, though certainly my complete recovery is an exceptional one, and I am happy in being able to assure those so unfortunate as to have dear ones needing the protection of such place, that they need feel no uncertainty of such receiving the kindest attention from the officers in your hospital for insane, and when leaving there myself after seven years, I felt indeed that I was leaving my home. With this exception, which lies within your power, gentlemen of the legislature, to remedy, the Hospital for the Insane of Indiana, embodies humanity in its truest sense.

Very sincerely,

"Non Compos Mentis."

CHAPTER XXVI.

The hospital for the insane, the inside workings of which I have attempted to give a truthful, unprejudiced history from the standpoint of a "patient" of seven years' experience, presents some features peculiar to itself and certainly deserving commendation as an example to other hospitals. In no other institution that I have visited have I found the patients so generally cheerful in appearance. Neither have I found a lovelier spot than the location and surroundings of the "Indiana State Hospital," situated three miles directly west of Indianapolis. It is connected with that city by street cars, making half hour trips. The grounds are beautifully laid out in ornamental walks, fountains and flowers. The lovely groves of splendid natural forest trees are interspersed with comfortable, brightly painted seats and hammocks for the comfort as well as the amusement of the patients, who are daily taken out of the wards for exercise, and last summer Dr. Flectcher added to his stock of amusements *foot balls*, which seemed in some cases to act almost as a tonic. Even the staidest old ladies there, who had heretofore resisted even the fascinations of the dance under the provokingly tempting music of "Hart's Band," could not resist the temptation to give that foot ball a kick as often as opportunity was given her.

A very amusing feature of the life there is the number of old ladies who so soon after their arrival there become dissipated, "fall from grace," so to speak. Very few of them object to attending the weekly dance, and after once going become so fascinated with the sport as not to be satisfied unless they, too, learn to dance. As a general thing these dances are quite orderly, as the rules require that the male attendants dance with the female patients and the female attendants with the male patients. And another marked peculiarity is that upon recovery they do not return to their old-timed prejudices against such innocent amusement, and I presume in many instances, upon their return home, their pious old husbands are dreadfully shocked over the evil ways into which their wives have fallen. I remember one little woman who laughed until she cried over her anticipated fun at her husband's horror when she should tell him she had learned to dance and drink beer at the asylum. "Why," she said, "my husband won't even buy me whisky for my camphor bottle, and won't he groan when I pretend I can't live without a keg of beer at my command."

During one period of my stay there eggnog was the prevailing tonic prescribed for the use of delicate patients. At another period beer was the prevailing strengthener, both of which were monopolized with the perfection of regularity by the delicate (?) attendants, since it was entirely too much trouble to force the patients to swallow *this* sort of medicine. My indignation got the better of my prudence upon one occasion, on this account, and I "reported my attendants," an "unpardonable sin" among the fraternity, and one I never ventured upon while in the asylum but twice, the last time being after I was very much "at myself," therefore not inclined to submit to the indignity of being "ordered out of the dining-room" where I was assisting with the work simply because I had contradicted a statement one of the attendants was making against me to the supervisoress, outrageously untruthful. After the supervisoress had gone my young lady ordered me to "walk out of the dining-room or she would call Miss K. (her partner) and they would put me out." Well, I walked out, since I had more pride then and self respect than to wish to get into a "fight" and give her the pleasure of using force against me, and the matter, as far as I was concerned, might have rested there only that she followed me to my room and said: "I'll have you understand there's a good deal of difference between you and I. You're nothing but a patient, and I'll not have such a nasty thing in my dining-room." I said

I have no aspirations toward your position, but you will find that "only being a patient" means something when I report your conduct to Dr. Thomas. From that day she was my enemy, tho' previous to that time I had upon more than one occasion befriended her. For several months before this the doctor had allowed me to sit up at night until the attendants retired, thinking by this I might more readily sleep, as I was so sleepless without "night medicine." I did not interfere with their comfort or privacy at all, but spent my evenings in the ward sitting-room either reading or sewing. One evening after the patients were all locked in their rooms and I was comfortably fixed with an interesting book, she walked in and said, "Now, madame, I want you to go this minute to bed. Dr. Thomas told me you should go to bed every night this week while I am alone (her partner was away for I week) when the other patients do." And I said, don't take your word for this Miss H. Last night the doctor asked me (since you had headache) if I would retire at the patients' hour, and I said I would. Certainly I would and did. You know very well that it was not necessary for you to have asked this of Dr. Thomas. You only did this for effect against me. Had you told me you had headache and asked me politely I would have gone to bed last night as freely for your request as his, but I will not to-night until my usual hour." Very well, madame, she said, I'll give you just ten minutes, and then I'll ring the telephone and Dr. Thomas will come up here and walk you off to your room faster than ever you went, and she continued, you 're so smart! I just wish Dr. Thomas would take you off this ward, and he would too if I would ask him to. Then I said: "Why don't you ask him then? And why don't you ring that telephone? This is about as suitable a time as we could wish to settle this matter. I don't believe the doctor said I was to go to bed every night this week at eight o'clock, and I dare you to send for him." Well, my interesting book was a failure that night. She forgot the dignity of her position and I presumed upon mine "nothing but a patient," and told her some

tolerably plain facts. After she had accused me of staying on
the ward against hers and her partner's wish on purpose to
have an opportunity of "playing the spy" and "reporting"
every thing they did, I said, Only that I know your
circumstances, and that you told me so yourself, that if you
should be discharged you had no home to go to, I would
report this interview not only to Dr. Thomas, but to Dr.
Fletcher, and they would sustain me if I am "nothing but a
patient." And I said further, I shall stay right here on the
fourth ward while I stay in this institution. And from this
night you shall treat me with the respect due me as a
woman—your superior in age at least—and I'll never submit
to another single impertinence from you! And from that time
she did treat me with politeness, and I wish her to understand
that whatever may have been her contrary belief, this is my
first "reporting" in that quarrel between us, and my
aspirations have not yet reached the height of becoming an
attendant.

I meet many persons who express surprise that I am not at all
sensitive regarding my insane experience, and others who
regard me a little doubtfully, as though possibly I may not
even yet be exactly level, and others again who are so
surprised and so very sure "you know," that nothing of the
kind will ever come to them, because nothing of that sort ever
was in "our family!" Nothing of what sort? Brains? In my own
case I have not the slightest fear of ever again becoming
insane; I feel perfectly sure of myself, a satisfaction I did not
once possess. Through past weakness I have become strong,
and I have come out of my wilderness of affliction a better
woman than I was when I professed to be a Christian. One
month after my discharge—at which time I visited my
children for the first time—I returned to my old home where I
was born. A visit affording both pain and pleasure. Friendly
hands were extended to welcome the wanderer home, and not
one word regarding my years of darkness that could offend or

jar upon a sensitive feeling, nothing but warmest love and sympathy, and as I stood again upon the banks of the beautiful Ohio, many far away scenes visible only to the resurrecting eye of memory passed before me, those of merry moonlight boat rides, of voices mingling in song and laughter, of girlish friendships formed when we counted not the past by its tears, and looked to the future for nothing but brightness. None of my school girl friends were left; some were in their peaceful beds in the quiet "grave-yard upon the hill," and all were scattered, in view of which I could truly realize the sad truth of a favorite song of my girlhood.

> "Many the changes since last we met,
> Blushes have brightened, tears have been wept;
> Friends have been scattered, like roses in bloom.
> Some at the bridal, some at the tomb."

But it was sweet coming home after all, and I remained there a month before returning for a short time to my other home — the asylum — before going to Aurora, Indiana — the home of my children — to enter suit for my right to see my children, and for my release from the tie which was now but a miserable mockery of marriage. The proceedings of that "compromise" are already public matter, much against my wish, as I had already been accused of "seeking notoriety," in going to my husband's home to see my children. Strange language to be used in regard to a mother's anxiety to see her children after years of cruel separation. Only the fact of my inability to care for those children, since my long affliction and hospital life, has unfitted me for many of the avenues of support sought for and within a woman's reach, prevented me testing the "majesty of the law" in behalf of the mother's right against the father who deserted and tried to disgrace his wife. My conduct and character need no vindication; I can afford to stand before the "bar of public opinion" upon my own merits, conscious of my entire innocence of any wrong toward my husband; neither have I come out of this contest a "social outcast;" I am secure in the possession of friends, true and tried, upon whom I can rely, and I claim no undeserved sympathy, neither have I any wish to pose before the public as a martyr. I have written these reminiscences of my peculiarly saddened life from different motives; partly, that it is a comfort and relief thus to give expression to my thoughts; partly, hoping for pecuniary assistance, but my purest, best motive, is the sincere hope of raising the drooping, hopeless spirit, and strengthening the fainting heart of some other miserable victim of this fearful horror, insanity; since certainly none should despair of recovery in view of my coming out "From under the Cloud."

> And so I penned
> It down until at last it came to be,
> For length and breadth, the bigness which you see,
> And some said print it, others said not so!
> Some said it might do good,
> Others said No! — JOHN BUNYAN.

WHAT IS THE VERDICT?

TESTIMONIALS.

College Hill, Ohio,
April 20, 1885.
To Mrs. Anna Agnew:
Dear Madame — I wish you abundant reward for all that you
may do in the line of enlightening the public on subjects
embraced in your work, and that you may yet find
compensation for some of the suffering you have endured.
Very respectfully,
Orpheus Everts.

Illinois Hospital for Insane,
Anna, III., April 18, 1886.
To Mrs. Anna Agnew:
My heart is ever a stronghold for afflicted humanity, but in all
my experience — over 21 years in the care of the insane — I call
no case to mind so deserving of sympathy and interest as that
of your own, which in condition, results and subsequent
domestic trials has been unique and peculiar. A detailed
account of your affliction, hospital experience, etc., will
certainly make a book worthy of public notice, and I predict
for it a successful sale.
Your friend, W. W. Hester.

LOGANSPORT, IND., April, 1886,
Mrs. Anna Agnew:
Dear Madame — I heartily wish your prospective literary
venture may be a success. Let me say that among the many
hundreds of my former patients I know of none so endowed
by nature and culture with the ability to tell the story which
your preface outlines. It will be a valuable contribution, not

only to general literature, but to the library of the Alienist.
I am very respectfully yours,
Joseph G. Rogers.

Indiana Hospital for Insane,
April 8, 1886.
Mrs. Anna Agnew:
My Dear Madame — You have my best wishes for success. The
experience you have had in hospitals for insane people, your
thoughts, acts, and observations of seven years placed before
the public, in the style of which I know you are capable, will,
beyond doubt, prove not only interesting but beneficial to the
people.
Very truly yours,
A. J. Thomas, Asst. Supt.

Indiana Hospital for Insane,
April 5, 1886.
To the Public:
I believe Mrs. Anna Agnew is permanently cured, because she
did not become doubly mad when the man who in the law
stands as her husband refused her the home that should have
welcomed her, and denied her the children which she had
bourne him. That she did not become homicidal at the sight of
such a man-monster is proof positive that reason and
judgment were fully restored.
W. B. Fletcher, Superintendent.

Pittsburg Commercial Gazette,
April 10, 1886.
Mrs. Anna Agnew:
Respected Madame — I wish you complete fulfillment of your
warmest hopes. Believe me, it is a powerful work, and

womanly nature will be powerless to resist this appeal for
humanity sake.
With the utmost respect, yours,
Chas. Harrison.

Made in the USA
Lexington, KY
14 September 2016